The Wholefood Pantry.

Amber Rose

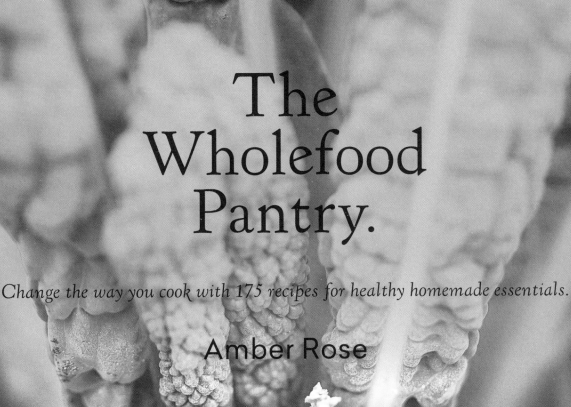

The Wholefood Pantry.

Change the way you cook with 175 recipes for healthy homemade essentials.

Amber Rose

The Wholefood Pantry.

Contents.

Introduction.

Kitchen staples and basics recipes are the nuts and bolts of every cook's kitchen. They are what I like to call the "toolbox" recipes. They are the flavorsome, nourishing base components, and they are also the things that can finish a dish to make it sing. In my kitchen they are essential go-to recipes that can be adapted throughout the year to create seasonal delicious meals, and satisfying bakes.

This is a reference book of all my favorite and most useful toolbox recipes. All the recipes are free from refined sugar, super healthy, delicious, and above all, easy to prepare.

The Wholefood Pantry is filled with all the recipes you will need to create healthy and beautiful syrups, chutneys, refined sugar-free jams, enzyme and probiotic-filled lacto pickles (ferments), cultured creams, healing broths, spice mixes, dips, nourishing desserts, nut milks, nut butters, sauces, essential marinades, irresistible raw chocolates, and so much more.

Armed with my simple, easy, and delicious toolbox recipes, you will be in control of what goes into your food, and how it is prepared. You will then naturally have the confidence to add seasonal ingredients to adapt and embellish your cooking and baking as the seasons change, to ensure maximum nutrition and flavor.

I grew up in New Zealand in a little wooden homemade house in the middle of a rambling orchard filled with wild flowers, heritage fruit trees, and a garden full of heritage vegetables. I spent my days as a young girl cooking and eating from the garden, and was endlessly appreciative of the sun-ripened fruits, and deliciously colorful and intensely flavored vegetables that made up my snacks and meals on a daily basis. I spent a lot of my childhood helping my mom in the garden and in the kitchen, harvesting fruits for jams, picking herbs for pesto, stirring bubbling pots of tomato sauce, picking rose petals for intoxicatingly fragrant wild rose petal jam, and scooping, peeling, and chopping all manner of colorful heritage produce that we made into preserves at various times of the year, to last through the seasons. When you have a garden, and not a row of supermarket aisles in front of you, you have to learn to cook and bake with what the seasons dictate, and to turn simple ingredients into beautiful, color-filled feasts. Cooking and eating seasonally means there are certain times of the year when vegetables or fruits are in abundance. It's during these times that mountains of basil get made into pesto, and popped in the freezer for use later in the year, or when the fruit that's dripping off the trees is made into pickles, chutneys, sauces, and other preserves.

Of course you don't need a garden to make all these wonderful "toolbox" delights. Although many of the recipes in this book are inspired by my childhood's seasonal, garden-to-table cooking experience, more often than not they can be whipped up in a flash with a minimum of ingredients and fuss. I have loved carrying on that approach to cooking even when, for many years, I lived in London, and didn't have a garden of my own.

The savory section contains the dips, pâtés, and other easy recipes that I go back to again and again. In the sweet section, the basic baking recipes are my old favorites that I love to adapt as the seasons change. They are so easy to whip up, that it's almost a sin, but for me, it's the simple things that always bring so much pleasure: baking my own loaf of bread, making my own jam, and whipping up nutritious desserts. I hope you find some pleasure and inspiration in these pages to help you fill your shelves and old jam jars full to the brim with delicious homemade toolbox delights.

Much Love,
Amber Rose xx

Nutrient-dense produce.

The words "nutrient dense" seem to have acquired a bit of buzz about them lately. It's a catchword we hear more and more, but with good reason: eating nutrient-dense produce is important for our health, and the health of generations to come.

Unfortunately, most of the food we buy from supermarkets has been bred for shelf life, and not nutrition. Often it is grown in mineral-deficient soils, or even worse, hydroponically (in polytunnels in water). On top of that, it has been treated with an array of chemicals and pesticides, then picked before it is ripe, so that it lasts longer on the shelf. This means the food has lower levels of disease-fighting nutrients in it, making it even less nutritious.

It can be hard to find nutrient-dense fruit and veggies, and also to maximize the nutrition of the produce you are eating, but here are a good few tips to help you on the way...

* Cut out processed food and refined food. These contain empty calories and do not nourish us.

* Buy local and in-season produce whenever you can. This will ensure fruit and veggies is naturally ripe, and hasn't been in cold storage for too long. Naturally tree-ripened fruit is more nutritious.

* Choose fruits and veggies grown from heritage seeds and trees. It is well-known that they are far more nutritious than their more modern options, which are usually bred for shelf life and looks.

* Choose dark-colored fruit and veggies, both of which contain increased amounts of antioxidants and minerals. Dark berries and dark green leaves are much more nutritious than their lighter colored counterparts.

* Buy organic food whenever you can. If money is an issue, at least try to get organic when buying produce that has thin, edible skin that isn't usually peeled—things like berries, peaches, tomatoes, etc. Non-organic versions will be covered in chemicals. Produce with thicker skins, like carrots and pineapples, is usually peeled before eating anyway, which will remove most of the chemicals. These chemicals will contribute to a damaged gut, a less effective immune system, and hormone issues, amongst other things. When plants have been grown in chemicals, there is no way that the soil can be healthy; if the soil is not healthy, then the plants will not be healthy, and so they will not make for nutritious food.

* Eat high levels of traditional, healthy fats and oils. We require a minimum of 1200 IU daily of naturally sourced Vitamin A, without which our bodies cannot absorb key minerals and vitamins. Eat your fruit and vedge alongside healthy fats: add good-quality cold-pressed oils to your salad dressings, and add cream, yogurt, or coconut cream to your fruit or desserts. Many of the vitamins and minerals in fruit and vedge are fat-soluble, so if you eat them with healthy fat, then you maximize your nutrient uptake.

* Try to always soak, sprout, or ferment your grains, seeds, nuts, and legumes. This will ensure that they nourish you fully, rather than leaching important minerals, vitamins, and enzymes from your body. Unsoaked, they are hard to digest, and actually contain toxic ingredients, which, over a long period of time, can have a detrimental effect on the entire body. Soaking, sprouting, or fermenting means you get as much goodness as possible out of them, which will in turn nourish you in the best possible way.

My top superfoods to boost immunity and well-being.

Having grown up in New Zealand with an incredible organic garden filled with heritage vegetables and fruits, flowers and herbs, and wild food in abundance, I then moved to one of the biggest cities in the world, London, where it seemed that the only superfoods available were those that lined a health-food store's shelves. After some time spent paying for expensive seaweeds, berries harvested from remote corners of the world, and pseudo cereals with price tags equivalent to extortion, I moved to the countryside, where I was promptly reminded that superfoods are all around us, local, and sometimes even free to forage.

Look around you, and find what is local to you. Not only will it be fresher and more potent, it will generally be cheaper, and probably more suited to what your body needs, as it will be seasonal. If you live in a city, go to farmers' markets, or research foraging courses that are hosted in nearby countryside.

Ignore the way the health industry has started marketing "superfoods" as a way of making big bucks. These are the real superfoods that you should look out for. It's common sense really—just look at what traditional cultures have been eating for thousands of years: the wisdom is all there.

Cold-pressed oils, coconut oil, olive oil, fish oil, nut and seed oil.
Cold-pressed oils give us immune benefiting components, antioxidants, and have substances that trigger the inflame/anti-inflame healing process and more.

Butter and ghee, from grass-fed cows (see pages 112-116).
Ghee and butter contain vitamin K2, which plays a crucial role in bone, facial, and dental development in growing babies and children. It also helps to heal the gut, reduces the risk of heart disease, and helps with weight loss.

Eggs from pastured organic chickens (see pages 66-70).
Eggs are amongst the most nutritious foods on the planet. They are packed full of healthy fats, protein, and essential vitamins.

Organic or wild dark leafy greens, fresh green herbs, stinging nettles and herbs, wild garlic leaves.
A treasure trove of nutrients, these act as antioxidants, and also alkalize the body. They cleanse and provide important minerals.

Bee pollen.
Bee pollen is considered to be one of nature's most complete foods. It's approximately 40 percent protein, in the form of free amino acids that are ready to be used directly by the body. It can reduce cravings and addictions, extend longevity, reduce allergies, help with infertility, and prevent infectious diseases.

Gelatin/bone broth, made from pastured organic chickens/animals or wild animals (see pages 136-140).
A powerful gut healer that deserves a place in your weekly diet.

Turmeric (see page 145).
Turmeric contains powerful medicinal properties, and has naturally-occuring anti-inflammatory compounds that help reduce inflammation. It also dramatically increases the antioxidant capacity within the body.

Onions and garlic
These contain extremely high amounts of prebiotics, which are what the good guys in our gut, the probiotics, feed on.

Nuts and seeds, eaten after soaking or sprouting.
Full of protein and heart-healthy fats. They also contain plenty of life-enhancing nutrients.

Dark berries, ideally wild or foraged.
Berries, such as elderberries, blueberries, and blackberries, contain very high amounts of antioxidants, and also help to heal the gut.

Fermented vegetables (see pages 145-153).
These contain huge amounts of probiotics and enzymes that boost immunity, help to heal the gut, and help with digestion.

Savory
Pantry.

My savory "toolbox" recipes are the recipes that have stood the test of time in my kitchen, year in, year out. They have traveled with me from country to country, many of them from my mother's kitchen to mine—they are the ones I go back to again and again. This section contains everything from gut-healing ferments through to nourishing bone broths, with fresh zingy salads, sauces, cultured creams, butters, and yogurts, as well as spice mixes and essential marinades. You will find everything you need to keep your fridge and pantry shelves stocked with delicious dips, oils, preserves, and easy-to-prepare flavor bombs all year-round.

An arugula and avocado salad
with salmon and toasted seeds.

SERVES 2

This is a meal in itself, perfect for a laid-back lunch or dinner. It's packed full of heart-healthy omegas 3 and 6, fiber, healthy fats, zinc, and various minerals, all of which boost the immune system, and keep you feeling satisfied, and ready for action. The fieriness of the arugula balances out the richness of the salmon, and the tamari dressing is just delicious. It contains ginger, which is anti-inflammatory, and great for the circulation too. Toasting the seeds enhances their nutty flavor—an essential step not to be skipped.

Preheat the oven to 350°F.

First make the dressing. Put all the ingredients in a jam jar, and screw on the lid tightly. Shake really well. Taste and season if you think it needs it—tamari is quite salty, so you may not need to.

Toast the sesame seeds in a dry skillet for a few minutes until golden. Place the salmon fillets on a baking sheet, spread with a little ghee, then sprinkle over the toasted sesame seeds, pop in the oven, and roast for about 12 minutes, or until the fish is just about cooked through. Salmon is lovely and tender if still a bit pink right in the middle. Once cooked, remove the fillets from the oven.

Meanwhile, toast the pumpkin and sunflower seeds. Spread them out on a baking sheet and pop in the oven for 6–8 minutes, or until they are just turning brown, and the pumpkin seeds are popping. Remove from the oven and set aside to cool.

To assemble the salad, simply arrange all the ingredients on a platter, flake over the fish, sprinkle over the toasted seeds and nori, then drizzle with the dressing. Enjoy.

FOR THE SALMON
2 tablespoons sesame
   seeds
2 salmon fillets (about
   5 ounces each), skin off
1 tablespoon ghee or
   olive oil
4½ tablespoons pumpkin
   seeds
⅓ cup sunflower seeds
1 sheet of toasted nori,
   broken up into little
   pieces

FOR THE DRESSING
3 tablespoons olive oil
Juice of 1 lemon
¼ teaspoon toasted
   sesame oil
½ teaspoon tamari
1 teaspoon finely grated
   fresh ginger (squeeze
   the pulp and discard,
   reserving the juice)
Sea salt and freshly
   ground black pepper

FOR THE SALAD
1 avocado, halved, pitted
   and the flesh scooped
   out in pieces
3 handfuls of arugula
2 scallions, finely sliced
1 zucchini, shaved
   lengthwise into ribbons

An alkalizing bowl of green goodness.
SERVES 2-3

This is a super-alkalizing green salad to balance the acid-forming effect of many processed foods that upset our digestive tract. Light, yet satisfying, it is very cleansing, which after too much rich food, is just what I feel like. The healthy fats of olive oil increase our vitamin absorption from the greens. There are a lot of fat-soluble vitamins present in the greens, so without the oil, we don't get the full benefit. This is such a simple salad with really pure flavors, so try to use the best-quality ingredients you can find. It is delicious on its own, or try it with a lovely piece of crispy salmon (see page 62) or some roast squash with a sprinkle of toasted pumpkin seeds for a heartier veggie meal. Yuzu is a Japanese citrus fruit—if you can't find yuzu, use a lovely organic lemon instead.

---

2 zucchini, washed
1 fennel bulb, trimmed, washed,
    and halved
½ cucumber, washed, lightly peeled
    if the skin is tough
A small bunch of dill, fronds torn

A small bunch of flat-leaf parsley,
    leaves picked and finely chopped
Extra virgin olive oil
Juice of 1 yuzu (or 1 lemon)
Sea salt and freshly ground black
    pepper

Shave the zucchinis lengthwise using a very sharp peeler until there is nothing left. Then do the same to the fennel bulb and cucumber.

Place the shaved greens into a bowl, sprinkle over the dill fronds and parsley. Give a light sprinkle with some really good-quality extra virgin olive oil, then squeeze over the yuzu juice, and season to taste.

My favorite jeweled green salad.

SERVES 3–4

This is my go-to quick and crunchy green salad, jewel-bright with pomegranate seeds. It's absolutely fantastic alongside almost anything—even scrambled eggs for breakfast. I keep the dressing in a jar, so that it's ready whenever I want a quick salad with my meal. It's my go-to dressing on just about any kind of salad.

FOR THE SALAD
2 baby gem lettuces, leaves
    separated and washed
Handful arugula, washed
1 avocado, halved and pitted
½ cucumber, peeled with some skin
    left on, halved lengthwise, then
    sliced into half moons
20 mint leaves, torn
2 tablespoons roughly chopped or
    torn flat-leaf parsley leaves
Seeds of ½ pomegranate

FOR THE CLASSIC FRENCH VINAIGRETTE
1 garlic clove, finely grated
1 heaping teaspoon Dijon mustard
Generous ⅓ cup cider vinegar
2 tablespoons lemon juice
1 teaspoon raw honey or
    coconut sugar
Generous ⅓ cup extra virgin olive oil
Sea salt and freshly ground black
    pepper to taste

First make the dressing. Put all the ingredients in a jam jar and screw on the lid tightly. Shake really well until everything is completely emulsified. Taste, and add a little more honey if it needs it.

Select a lovely serving bowl, put in the lettuce leaves and arugula, then using a teaspoon, scoop in the avocado, scatter over the cucumber, and lastly, sprinkle over the herbs and pomegranate seeds.

Dress the salad with the dressing (you won't need all of it but it keeps well for a week for another few salads). Give it a light and gentle mix and serve immediately.

Winter salad with a creamy cashew and preserved lemon dressing.

SERVES 4-6

Here is a colorful, warming, hearty salad for colder months. The sweetness of the squash goes so beautifully with the sharpness and creaminess of the preserved lemon dressing. Preserved lemons are lacto-fermented, which means they contain loads of naturally occurring probiotics to give your immune system a boost, just when it is most needed during the shorter days of autumn and winter, which is also when squash are in season and at their best.

FOR THE SALAD
1 large butternut squash (or your favorite variety of squash)
4 tablespoons ghee or olive oil
1 tablespoon sunflower seeds
1 tablespoon pumpkin seeds
1 tablespoon black sesame seeds
2 tablespoons slivered almonds
⅓ cup basil leaves
A handful of arugula
½ pomegranate, seeds removed and rinsed
Salt and freshly ground black pepper

FOR THE CASHEW AND PRESERVED LEMON DRESSING
1¼ cups cashews, soaked
2 tablespoons chopped preserved lemons (see page 151, or use store-bought)
Generous ¾ cup almond milk
Sea salt and freshly ground black pepper

To make the dressing simply put all the ingredients into a bowl and blitz with a stick blender, adding more almond milk if you require a thinner consistency for drizzling, or less for a dip. Season to taste, and set aside while you prepare the salad.

Preheat the oven to 425°F.

Trim the base and top off the squash, then cut it in half lengthwise. Use a spoon to remove the seeds. Cut each half into wedges about 1¼ inches thick.

Arrange the wedges on a roasting pan, skin-side down. Brush with ghee or olive oil, and season well with salt and pepper. Roast for 30–35 minutes. Keep an eye on the wedges—depending on your oven, they may take a little longer or a little less, but you don't want them to burn.

When the wedges are just catching at the edges and feel tender all the way through when poked with a knife, remove the pan from the oven and allow to cool.

Reduce the oven temperature to 350°F and put all the seeds and the almonds onto a clean baking sheet. Pop into the oven to toast for 6–8 minutes, or until lightly browned and popping.

When you are ready to assemble the salad, arrange the squash on a beautiful serving platter, sprinkle over the toasted seeds, almonds, basil, arugula, and pomegranate seeds, then serve with the dressing on the side. As a final flourish, you can drizzle with extra virgin olive oil, and add an extra sprinkle of sea salt and freshly cracked black pepper.

My classic summery tomato salad with a basil and lime dressing.

SERVES 3-4

I have wonderful memories of my childhood, wandering through my mom's heritage vegetable garden, and in particular the tomato patch. Mom grew about 20 different varieties of tomatoes, which all had to be hand-pollinated with tiny paintbrushes by us so they would not crossbreed. They came in all shapes, sizes and an array of colors—red, orange, yellow, green, and black, even striped—and all were unbelievably delicious, especially when freshly plucked off the vine on a hot summer's day, wrapped in a freshly picked basil leaf and popped straight into our mouths, warm from the sun, fragrant and perfectly delicious. Mom had tomatoes that were specifically for stuffing, some were for making sun-dried tomatoes or paste, while others were great for salads, and ones like the beefsteak were amazing in sandwiches and burgers. This easily thrown together summery salad always reminds me of those beautiful juicy tomatoes I grew up with. The dressing is the perfect accompaniment: piquant, full of flavor, and really brings out the sweetness of the tomatoes. The dressing would also work really well on any green salad—I usually tip up the salad bowl when the salad has been eaten and drink the leftover dressing, it's that good!

FOR THE SALAD
14 ounces tomatoes (a mix of colors and sizes)
½ red onion, thinly sliced
A small bunch of flat-leaf parsley, leaves picked and roughly chopped or torn
A small bunch of basil, roughly chopped or torn
Chive or arugula flowers (optional)

FOR THE DRESSING
Generous ¾ cup extra virgin olive oil
Generous ¾ cup freshly squeezed lime juice (about 4 limes)
2 teaspoons unrefined cane or coconut sugar
1 tablespoon finely chopped basil leaves
½ teaspoon Dijon mustard
Sea salt and freshly ground black pepper

First make the dressing. Put all the ingredients in a jam jar, and screw on the lid tightly. Shake really well until everything is completely emulsified.

To make the salad, cut up the tomatoes, arrange them on a platter, and sprinkle over the onion and herbs. If you have any chive or arugula flowers, sprinkle some of those over too. Drizzle over the dressing—you won't need all of it but it keeps well for a week for another few salads.

Enjoy the dressed salad immediately.

Crisp and crunchy chopped salad
with a creamy tahini dressing.

SERVES 3–4 AS A SIDE

I love a chopped salad, and this one has a pleasing contrast of crunchy ingredients and velvety-smooth creamy dressing. It's a good one to eat at lunchtime. because the healthy fats in the dressing keep your brain powered up for the afternoon, while simultaneously helping your body to absorb all the fat-soluble vitamins from the salad. If you wanted to add some protein, you could serve this salad with a crispy-skin fillet of fish from page 62 or some grilled chicken breast or vedge-loaded burger patties (see page 59). For a veggie option, try pan-frying some tempeh in coconut oil and a little tamari: simple and tasty.

FOR THE SALAD
1 large romaine lettuce, chopped
A handful of cherry tomatoes, halved
½ cucumber, peeled and diced
½ red onion, thinly sliced
A handful of French breakfast radishes, sliced
A handful of flat-leaf parsley leaves, finely chopped

FOR THE DRESSING
2 tablespoons tahini
¼ cup boiling water
1 garlic clove, finely grated or minced
½ cup plain yogurt or milk kefir (sheep or goat milk yogurt is fine)
3 tablespoons freshly squeezed lemon juice

First make the dressing. Stir the tahini and the water together in a bowl until smooth. Allow to cool. Add the remaining ingredients, and stir to combine.

Put the lettuce in a large salad bowl. Add the remaining salad ingredients, and toss gently to lightly mix.

Spoon over just enough of the dressing to lightly coat the salad. You may not need it all. It will keep in the fridge for a good week if there is any left.

This salad is also super delicious with the Classic French Vinaigrette on page 20.

Radicchio salad with sweet grilled pears and goat cheese.

SERVES 4 AS A SIDE

This salad is beautiful with my blackberry and elderberry vinaigrette—the berry-infused flavors really bring the fruit in the salad to life. The combination of the bitter salad leaves with the sweetness of the pears and the creamy goat cheese is sublime.

---

2 pears, peeled, cored and halved, then cut into 6 slices lengthwise
A large handful of blanched hazelnuts
2 tablespoons maple syrup
1 large round head purple radicchio, leaves separated

Scant 2 ounces soft, crumbly goat cheese
A handful of fresh blackberries, sliced in half lengthwise
Blackberry and elderberry vinaigrette (see right)

Place a cast-iron ridged grill pan over high heat, and lay the slices of pear onto the pan. Cook for 1–2 minutes on each side, or until nicely lined, but not overcooked or burnt. Remove the slices from the pan, and set aside to cool.

Next, tip the nuts into a small dry skillet that has been preheated over medium heat. Allow them to toast for a bit and get some color, then stir in the maple syrup, coating the nuts. Keep stirring until the syrup thickens—be careful not to let it burn, but leave it long enough to turn a darker color, and develop a stronger smell. Remove the nuts from the heat, and tip them onto a waiting plate, allowing them to cool a little.

Tear up the radicchio leaves, and put them onto a lovely platter. Scatter over the grilled pears, crumble over the goat cheese, and sprinkle over the halved blackberries. Roughly chop the cold and hardened nuts, and sprinkle them over the salad. Then gently sprinkle over enough blackberry vinaigrette to coat the salad.

Blackberry and elderberry vinaigrette.

MAKES 1¼ CUPS

Drizzle over hearty autumn salads with bitter leaves and autumn fruits, such as the radicchio salad, left.

⅔ cup extra virgin olive oil
⅔ cup blackberry and elderberry vinegar (see page 155)
½ teaspoon Dijon mustard

½ teaspoon raw honey or coconut sugar
Sea salt and freshly ground black pepper

Put all the ingredients in a jam jar and screw on the lid tightly. Shake really well. This vinaigrette keeps well at room temperature for at least a couple of weeks.

Variation: Raspberry vinaigrette.
As above, but replace the blackberry and elderberry vinegar with raspberry vinegar (see page 155).

A glorious paneer for all occasions.

SERVES 2-3

Homemade paneer is truly one of life's great pleasures: fluffy and light, satisfying and so delicious—a far cry from the unpleasant rubbery packs you can buy in the supermarkets. Somehow this simple fresh-tasting cheese just hits the spot, and it's very easy to make with no special equipment. Paneer is fantastic as a main dish for vegetarians and meat-eaters alike, but I also use it to top soups, dahl, and curries—you can even make desserts with it.

EQUIPMENT	FOR THE PANEER
1 cheesecloth, for straining the cheese	2 quarts + ½ cup organic whole milk
1 colander	18 ounces full-fat organic yogurt (homemade or store bought) or cow's milk kefir (see pages 120–121)
1 large mixing bowl	

Use the cheesecloth to line the colander and place over the mixing bowl.

Set a large pan over high heat, and pour in the milk, stirring every so often, keeping an eye on it as it can boil over very easily, which creates an awful mess. You want the milk to reach almost boiling point, then start to add the yogurt, one-third at a time. Don't stir too much or you will break up all the curds. When all the yogurt is added, you will notice the milk starting to turn to curds and whey. If this does not happen, you may need a bit more yogurt, or the milk may not be hot enough.

When the milk has completely separated into curds and whey, pour the whole lot into the lined colander. Pull up the sides of the cloth, and lift it out of the colander to let the curds drain a bit. Now give the enclosed curds a gentle squeeze, so that the excess whey runs into the bowl—but be careful, they're hot!

Next you want to wrap the curds up nicely in the cloth, and place them on a flat surface that can allow the curds to drain for the next step. I usually place the cloth-wrapped curds on the draining board of my sink.

The final step is to put a plate on top of the curds (or use the pot you cooked them in if it's nice and heavy). Either set a couple of unopened cans on top of the plate to weigh it down, or just press with your hands. Alternatively, drain off the whey into a clean jar (reserve it for later use) and set the full jar on the plate or in the pot. The length of time the curds drain affects the final texture: leave for 20 minutes for a more solid paneer, or for 5 minutes for a lighter, fluffier paneer. Both taste delicious; the density is a little different, but either creates a solid block of paneer.

At this point you can cut the paneer into steaks, season and fry, or you can chop it into little cubes and serve it on top of dahl, crumble it into soups, whatever you like really.

For paneer steaks see page 32.

Paneer steaks.

SERVES 3

Paneer steaks are incredibly simple and totally addictive. I actually find myself craving these sometimes. They make a great dish for vegetarians as paneer is full of protein. If you fancy a quick lunch or dinner, and don't have any spice mix on hand, you can keep the steaks plain as I often do—they are delicious both ways.

---

1 quantity of fresh paneer
  (see page 28)
A knob of ghee

1½ teaspoons biryani spice mix,
  or one of the Spice Mixes from
  pages 104–108 (optional)

Cut the paneer into three steaks. Sprinkle with the biryani spice mix, if using. Place a medium skillet over medium heat. Add the ghee, and when it's warmed, gently add the paneer steaks. Allow them to cook for 1–2 minutes on each side. They catch easily, and cook quickly, so keep an eye on them. When they are done, slip them out of the pan and serve with my jeweled green salad on page 20.

Mung dahl with celeriac.

SERVES 4-6

This is my go-to dahl—super cleansing, nourishing, and really easy to make. A very good friend of mine, Michelle, passed on this recipe to me and it's insanely good. I have taken it one step further by adding wilted spinach and optional paneer. The ghee and spices have a deeply nourishing and cleansing effect on the body's cells—ghee is a very healthy fat and the spices each have their own unique healing abilities. The ginger is anti-inflammatory, which also helps our immune systems. Mung beans contain loads of fiber, which is great for digestion, and their earthy flavor is picked up by the celeriac.

You can serve this quite thick, like a classic dahl, or water it down a bit and serve it more like a soup. It's really good just as it is, or you can top it with cubed paneer and wilted spinach for a more substantial meal. This Ayurvedic dahl is traditionally served with organic white rice, which is easier to digest than brown rice, or try it with cauliflower rice (see page 49).

Set a large heavy-bottomed pan over medium heat, add the ghee, and when it's hot, add the onions and leek. Fry them for about 10 minutes, or until softened, but not browned. Add the spices, bay leaves, and ginger, and continue to stir for 1–2 minutes, or until the spices become fragrant.

Add the mung beans and celeriac, continue to stir and cook for an additional 1–2 minutes. Add 6¼ cups of water or whey, or a mixture, and bring to a boil, then turn the heat down, and simmer very gently for about 1 hour. Add more water as the dahl simmers, depending on what consistency you would like it. When it's cooked, season to taste.

To make the spinach, set a medium skillet over medium heat, allow the pan to warm up, then add the ghee, mustard seeds, and curry leaves. When they begin to pop and sizzle, add the spinach and keep stirring—it will wilt down very quickly. Baby spinach will only take 30 seconds–1 minute at most; bigger leaves, kale, or cavolo nero may need an additional minute. Season to taste, and serve on top of your dahl, with cubed paneer, if you wish.

For Cauliflower Rice see page 49.

FOR THE DAHL
5 tablespoons ghee
3 medium onions, finely chopped
1 leek, finely chopped
1 teaspoon ground fennel
2 teaspoons ground coriander
2½ teaspoons ground cumin
1 teaspoon ground turmeric
2 bay leaves
2½ tablespoons finely grated ginger
14 ounces mung beans, soaked overnight, or for a few hours, drained
A handful or two of celeriac root, peeled and grated

Sea salt and freshly ground black pepper
6¼–8½ cups filtered water, or spring water, or whey from making paneer

FOR THE SPINACH
A knob of ghee
1 teaspoon black mustard seeds
A few curry leaves
A couple handfuls fresh spinach, kale, or cavolo nero, tough stalks removed
Sea salt and freshly ground black pepper to taste

Cubed paneer (see page 28) to serve

Eggplant roasted with sumac and cherry tomatoes.

SERVES 4

This is a super-easy and stunning way to serve eggplant. Slow-roasting them really brings out their flavor, and the toppings add classic Middle-Eastern notes. You could serve this with some broiled or roast lamb, some merguez sausages, or on its own as a beautiful and delicious vegetarian main course.

2 large eggplants
2 tablespoons ghee or
   olive oil
1 tablespoon sumac
   powder
10 ounces cherry
   tomatoes on the vine
1 quantity of kale and
   walnut pesto (see page
   88)

Lemon juice (optional)
Olive oil (optional)
A handful of arugula
   leaves
Seeds from ½
   pomegranate
Sea salt and freshly
   ground black pepper

Preheat the oven to 425°F.

Cut the eggplant in half lengthwise and score the flesh in a criss-cross pattern. Rub the flesh generously with the ghee, and sprinkle over some salt and pepper, and the sumac. Place on a baking sheet, skin-side down, and roast for about 35 minutes.

Remove from the oven and place 4–5 cherry tomatoes, still on the vine, on top of each eggplant half. Return to the oven and roast for an additional 10–15 minutes, or until the cherry tomatoes are blistering and cooked.

Scoop each half eggplant onto a platter and drizzle over the pesto. If it's too thick to drizzle, thin it down with some extra lemon juice and/or olive oil. Sprinkle over the arugula leaves and pomegranate seeds. Serve.

Roasted baby carrots with gremolata.

SERVES 3-4

This is a truly delicious way of serving little tender baby carrots. It would make a tasty side dish with roast chicken or rare roast beef, or served with some guacamole and a crisp green salad. Gremolata is an Italian flavoring that can be sprinkled over many things, before or after cooking—everything from baked fish to avocado on toast. It's a wonderful ingredient to have on hand, a real flavor bomb, and really easy to make, not to mention very nutritious.

A few handfuls of baby
   carrots
Ghee or olive oil

1 quantity of gremolata
   (see page 104)
Sea salt and freshly
   ground black pepper

Preheat the oven to 350°F.

Leave about ¾ inch of the stalks on the baby carrots. Give them a good scrub, but there's no need to peel. Spread them out on a baking sheet, and sprinkle with a couple of tablespoons of ghee or olive oil.

Roast for about 35 minutes, or until tender and cooked.

Remove from the oven, transfer the carrots to a serving platter, season with salt and pepper, sprinkle over the gremolata, and serve.

SAVORY PANTRY Salads *Vegetables and Sides* Meat and Fish Eggs Flavored Yogurts Mayonnaise Sauces Salsa and Chutneys

Roasted beets with green oil.

SERVES 5-6 AS A SIDE

Roasting beets really brings out their deep, sweet earthiness. The green oil drizzled over the top is simply divine, and cuts the sweetness of the beets with a grassy freshness. You could serve these just as they are as a side dish, or make them the hero of a salad. I love these beets with a soft-boiled egg, peeled and halved, with a few watercress leaves. Quail eggs would also be delicious.

5 medium beets
1 quantity soft green herb oil (see page 119)
A handful of toasted pumpkin seeds
A handful of arugula
Sea salt and freshly ground black pepper

Preheat the oven to 350°F.

Wash the beets, trim off the stalks without cutting into the beets, then wrap them in foil. Place them in a roasting dish and pop into the oven for about 1 hour. To test if they are fully cooked, poke a sharp knife into the center of a beet; it should feel tender all the way through.

Unwrap the beets, being careful of the hot steam that will escape. Allow them to cool a little, then carefully peel the skin off the beets—it should slip off quite easily.

Cut the peeled beets into wedges and scatter onto a serving platter. Generously spoon over the green oil, give it a sprinkle of salt, and a few twists of pepper. Scatter over the pumpkin seeds and arugula, and serve.

Zucchini noodles and ribbons.

SERVES 2

When I discovered how easy it was to create gluten-free vegetable noodles and ribbons from zucchini, it was a revelation. You can add these noodles to soups, use them as a base for Bolognese (see page 58), or my favorite tomato sauce (see page 84) for a quick tomato pasta. You can also turn them into a salad by adding fresh tomatoes, pine nuts, torn basil, shaved Parmesan cheese, and a drizzle of oil—really the possibilities are endless, and they are all tasty, not to mention nutrient-dense and incredibly good for you.

My son's favorite way of eating "zoodles" is just as they are in this recipe, topped with garlicky Mediterranean prawns, a squeeze of lemon, and plenty of chopped parsley. You will need a good spiralizer to make these noodles, though, it's essential. For the ribbons, you can use a sharp peeler, preferably a swivel-headed one, unless you have a spiralizer with a shaving attachment. The ribbons are great lightly warmed in a skillet, and then topped with a fried egg and anything else you might fancy for a cooked breakfast, perhaps some garlic mushrooms, or roast cherry tomatoes.

I find zucchini noodles a bit plain served completely bare, so here I jazz them up a bit to create a more delicious base for your toppings.

2 zucchini, topped and tailed (I allow 1–2 medium zucchini per person)
A drizzle of olive oil
A squeeze of lemon
Sea salt and freshly ground black pepper
A pinch of dried red pepper flakes (optional)
A scattering of chive flowers, if you have them (optional)

To make noodles, spiralize the zucchini according to your machine's instructions. Place the noodles into a mixing bowl, drizzle them with olive oil, squeeze over some lemon juice, and add a good pinch of sea salt, and a few twists of black pepper. For a bit of extra kick, add a pinch of red pepper flakes.

Give the noodles a good toss, and then top them with whatever you fancy... meatballs, ragù, garlic prawns, oven-roasted cherry tomatoes, pesto, roast veggies and Parmesan cheese—the choice is yours.

To make ribbons, use a good-quality sharp peeler and, using quite a light touch, shave the zucchini lengthwise from top to bottom. When you are halfway through the zucchini, you can turn it and start from the other side. This will give you thinner ribbons but that's okay, it looks pretty. Put the ribbons in a bowl, and toss with the remaining ingredients. They are now ready to top with whatever you fancy.

Pumpkin stuffed with kale pesto and mozzarella.

SERVES 6–8

This is comfort food at its best! I have my dear friend Tania to thank for it. She lived for ten years in Venezuela, where it's a staple dish. It's a genius way of serving pumpkin, and kids will love it! I'm a huge fan of pumpkin—I crave its comforting, golden nutty flesh when the leaves start to fall from the trees, and the evenings are cooler. My mom grew all sorts of varieties of pumpkins and squash, and I loved them from a young age. The nutty, drier-fleshed ones were my favorite as they were the perfect vehicle for lashings of homemade butter and salt. For this recipe, try to find pumpkins that don't have a very moist flesh when cooked as the pesto and mozzarella will supply more than an ample amount of cheesy, tasty, and moist deliciousness. Also, I recommend you use best-quality buffalo mozzarella. I find that cow's mozzarella, although cheaper, releases a lot of liquid during cooking, which is not a good thing for this recipe, as it makes the pumpkin flesh watery. If this does happen, drain off the liquid and carry on cooking—it will still be delicious.

---

2 small round pumpkins or winter squash (about 14 ounces each)
1 quantity of Kale and Cashew Pesto (see page 88)

2 mozzarella balls, preferably buffalo

Give the pumpkins a good wash, scrubbing off any dirt. Now carefully cut a circle into the top of each pumpkin so that you can then lift it off like a lid. It's best if you can cut the circle on a bit of an angle, so that as the pumpkin cooks and shrinks slightly, the lid has a lip to sit on, which will prevent it falling into the center. Reserve the lids, and scoop out and discard all the seeds from the interior with a spoon.

Place the pumpkins on a baking sheet, and spoon 4 tablespoons of pesto into each cavity, then pop a mozzarella ball into each one and replace the lids. Put the sheet into the hot oven, and bake for 1 hour. Remove from the oven, and take off the lids, then pop the sheet back into the oven, and continue cooking for another 20 minutes, or until the cheese is melted and bubbling. Remove from the oven, replace the lids again, and serve immediately, whole, or cut into wedges.

Depending on the size and variety of your pumpkins, cooking times can vary considerably, so just test for doneness using a sharp knife. If the flesh is tender all the way through, and the cheese has melted, then the pumpkins are ready to go.

Oven fries with rosemary and garlic.

SERVES 4-6 AS A SIDE

Sometimes all you need in life is a plate of fries. My mom used to cook great fries, made with beautiful potatoes from her garden, sprinkled with rosemary from the herb patch, and a generous sprinkle of sea salt: heaven!

We didn't have tomato sauce in our house when I was growing up. Instead we had my mom's delicious homemade plum ketchup (see page 79). There's also my recipe on page 86 for homemade probiotic ketchup. Because it's fermented, it contains probiotics, the friendly yeasts and bacteria that our gut needs to stay healthy, which in turn boosts our immunity.

5 tablespoons ghee
2 large sweet potatoes, unpeeled and scrubbed
1 large potato, unpeeled and scrubbed
¼ medium-sized celeriac, peeled
2 sprigs of rosemary
1 bulb of garlic, separated into cloves but skins left on
Sea salt and freshly ground black pepper

TO SERVE
Any or all of the following:
Probiotic ketchup (see page 86)
Plum ketchup (see page 79)
Homemade aioli, sriracha, or saffron mayo, or any mayo that takes your fancy (see pages 73–74)

Preheat the oven to 375°F..

Put 4 tablespoons of the ghee into a large roasting pan with shallow sides and place it into the oven to heat.

Cut the sweet potatoes, potato, and celeriac into long French fry-sized pieces. Place them in a bowl, and toss in the remaining tablespoon of ghee, then lay them in the preheated roasting pan—be careful as the ghee will be hot. Sprinkle over the rosemary and garlic cloves. Make sure the fries are in a single layer, or they won't crisp up.

Return the hot pan to the oven, and roast for 40–50 minutes, turning the fries over halfway through.

When the fries are golden, and just starting to catch at the edges, remove them from the oven, and enjoy with the ketchup and aioli just as they are, or served with the rest of your meal.

Try using one of the flavored salts on page 111 for a different flavor boost.

Roasted red onions to go with anything.

SERVES 4-6 AS A SIDE

These beautiful rings of deep purple deliciousness lend a superb depth of flavor and color to many dishes. They are both sharp and sweet at the same time, and are insanely good tossed into salads, served with roast meats, added to sandwiches, or as a topping for vegetarian mains. They are a great thing to have up your sleeve, to bring a bit of excitement to a dish that needs enlivening.

8–10 medium red onions, peeled
6½ tablespoons maple syrup
scant 1 cup balsamic vinegar
⅓ cup ghee or olive oil
Sea salt and freshly ground black pepper

Preheat the oven to 350°F.

Cut the onions into slices about ⅛-inch thick. Spread them out in a single layer on a large baking sheet. Drizzle first with the maple syrup and balsamic vinegar, then the ghee or olive oil. Roast for 30 minutes, turning them halfway through. When they are done, they should look deep purple and glistening; give them a few more minutes if they are not yet yielding and starting to caramelize.

Serve warm or cold. Best eaten the day they are cooked.

Slow-roasted tomatoes.

SERVES 4

These bright red little parcels of joy lend both flavor and color to many dishes. They are softer and less chewy than sun-dried tomatoes, of which I am not much of a fan. Roasting really intensifies the flavor of these beauties—they work really well with fish, red meat, and salads. They also go beautifully with cheeses, especially goat cheeses and ricotta. Warm from the oven, they are incredible with soft scrambled eggs and plenty of chopped chives. I like to make a big batch, and keep any that are left over under olive oil in the fridge for adding to a cheese course or sandwich (they will last for about a week under oil).

20–30 baby plum tomatoes
1 tablespoon coconut sugar
A pinch of red pepper flakes
1 teaspoon fennel seeds
½ teaspoon thyme leaves
A squeeze of lemon juice
Sea salt and freshly ground black pepper

Preheat the oven to 225°F and line a baking sheet with baking parchment.

Halve the tomatoes lengthwise and lay them in a single layer, cut-side up, on the prepared baking sheet. Mix together the rest of the ingredients, except the lemon juice, with a good hearty pinch of salt, and about ten twists of the pepper grinder. Sprinkle the mixture over the cut tomatoes, squeeze over the lemon juice, pop them in the oven, and leave undisturbed for 3–4 hours. They should shrivel to some degree and yet remain moist. Remove from the oven, and set aside until ready to use.

These delicious and intensely flavored tomatoes will keep in the fridge for 4–5 days.

Sweet potato hasselbacks.

SERVES 4

These are crispy roasties prepared Swedish-style, but here I'm using sweet potatoes (in New Zealand we call them "kumara") instead of ordinary potatoes. I have served them with an avocado salad and shavings of Parmesan, but I have been known to top them with meatballs in tomato sauce—even beans and cheese. They are good any which way you serve them.

---

4 medium sweet potatoes, washed
4 small knobs of butter (2–3½ tablespoons each), softened
Olive oil
Leaves from 4 thyme sprigs
½ teaspoon sumac
Sea salt and freshly ground black pepper

Preheat the oven to 350°F.

Place the sweet potatoes lengthwise on a chopping board. Starting at one end and using a sharp knife, carefully cut about three-quarters of the way through the width—be careful not to go too far, or you will cut off slices. Repeat, making the cuts quite close together, keeping the potatoes intact at the base, all along the length of the potatoes.

Lay the potatoes in an ovenproof dish just big enough to fit them all in a single layer. Rub the butter over the tops, carefully pushing it down the slits. Drizzle over a generous amount of olive oil, sprinkle over the thyme leaves and sumac, and season.

Transfer to the oven and bake on the middle rack for about 40 minutes, or until the potatoes are just catching at the edges, and soft all the way through.

Serve piping hot with your favorite sides or toppings.

For a flavor bomb, try sprinkling one of my Spice Mixes (see pages 104-108) in place of the sumac and thyme.

Mushrooms with a hazelnut, thyme, and pecorino crumble.

SERVES 4-6 AS A SIDE

Pure comfort for those colder autumn days, this dish can be a vegetarian main, or it could be served alongside a roast chicken and green salad. The crumble topping adds a pleasing crunch.

¾ cup hazelnuts
1⅛ sticks unsalted butter
7 ounces portobello mushrooms, cleaned and cut into thick strips
7 ounces chanterelles, cleaned
A small bunch of flat-leaf parsley, leaves picked and roughly chopped
A small bunch of fresh thyme, leaves only
½ lemon
⅔ cup finely grated pecorino cheese
Sea salt and freshly ground black pepper

Preheat the oven to 350°F. Spread out the hazelnuts on a baking sheet, and roast for about 8 minutes, or until they are lovely and golden. Take out of the oven, and rub them in a clean dishtowel to remove most of the skins. Divide the nuts into two equal portions, finely grind half in a food processor, and roughly chop the other half. Set aside.

Set a large skillet over quite high heat, and add half the butter to the pan. When the butter is sizzling, add the mushrooms, give them a quick toss and allow them to sizzle without stirring too much (stirring them releases too much liquid and they will become soggy). After 2 minutes, turn them over to cook on the other side. When they are tender and nearly cooked, add the parsley, 1 teaspoon of thyme leaves and a good squeeze of lemon juice. Sprinkle with salt and black pepper, and give one last stir. Scoop the mushrooms into a roasting dish that holds them snugly, without too much room. They can be piled up a little.

Preheat the broiler to medium. Mix the remaining butter with the finely ground nuts, add 1 teaspoon of thyme leaves, salt, and pepper, then mix in the roughly chopped nuts, and lastly the cheese. Sprinkle the crumble mix over the mushrooms and place under the broiler for 2–3 minutes, or until nicely browned. Serve while hot.

My favorite 3-root smash with roasted garlic and chives.

SERVES 4

This smash is addictive, creamy, delicious, colorful, and has a great chunky texture, perfect for topping with all manner of things. I top it with everything from roast meat and sausages, through to garlicky greens with a crispy fried egg. It's totally comforting, and a great winter warmer, wholesome and filling.

1 bulb of garlic, kept whole

2 tablespoons ghee

4–5 large carrots, peeled and cut into 1¼-inch chunks

⅓ rutabaga, peeled and cut into 1¼-inch chunks

½ celeriac, peeled and cut into 1¼-inch chunks

7 tablespoons unsalted butter

A small bunch of chives, roughly chopped

Sea salt and freshly ground black pepper

Preheat the oven to 400°F.

Cut the garlic bulb in half horizontally, place it on a large sheet of foil, drizzle with the ghee, and season with salt and black pepper. Wrap the foil around the garlic, and place on a baking sheet in the oven for 40 minutes until golden and soft.

Place the carrots, swede, and celeriac in a large pan of lightly salted water, and bring to a boil. Simmer for 20 minutes until soft, then drain and allow to cool in the colander for 5 minutes.

Return the carrots, swede, and celeriac to a clean saucepan. Squeeze in half the roasted garlic (discarding the papery skins, and keeping the other half for another recipe), and add the butter. Using either a fork or a masher, mash the root vegetables until you have a rough, chunky consistency. Add salt and pepper to taste.

Spoon the mash into a serving bowl, scatter over the chives, and serve while piping hot.

Whole roasted spiced cauliflower.

SERVES 4

This is a stunning and delicious vegetarian main dish. You can keep it simple or you can spice it up and really go to town for a decadent festive treat. It's perfect for a Sunday roast and beautiful enough for a vegetarian Christmas main.

FOR THE MARINADE
1 lemon, juice only for the marinade (zest added later in the cooking)
A few sprigs of thyme, leaves only
2–3 tablespoons olive oil or ghee
1 teaspoon honey
4–5 cloves of garlic, peeled
1 teaspoon smoked paprika
1 teaspoon sumac
A few twists of freshly ground black pepper
A generous pinch of sea salt

FOR THE CAULIFLOWER
1 large cauliflower
4 tablespoons dry Marsala wine
14 ounces cherry tomatoes
A few whole sprigs of thyme
½ cup slivered almonds, lightly toasted
2 tablespoons pumpkin seeds, lightly toasted
½ bunch flat-leaf parsley, leaves torn
Extra virgin olive oil

Preheat the oven to 350°F.

Blitz all the ingredients for the marinade in a food processor, just enough until they come together in a rough, chunky paste—you don't want it totally smooth.

Trim the outer leaves and stalk from the base of the cauliflower, so that it can sit beautifully flat. You can discard the leaves, or use them in a veggie stockpot if they are still perky. Rub the marinade over the entire cauliflower, then place it in an ovenproof dish with a lid. I like to use my heavy-bottomed casserole dish. Sprinkle over the Marsala, and put the lid on the dish.

Transfer the dish to the oven, and cook for about 1 hour, or until tender. It may need an additional 10–15 minutes, depending on the size of your cauliflower.

Remove the dish from the oven, and scatter over the cherry tomatoes, thyme sprigs and the reserved lemon zest. Turn the oven up to 425°F, and return the dish to the oven without the lid for an additional 15 minutes, or until the cauliflower has a lovely golden crust.

When the cauliflower is ready, remove it from the oven, scatter over the toasted almonds, pumpkin seeds, and parsley leaves, and spoon over some of the juices from the bottom of the pan. Drizzle over some extra virgin olive oil, and grind over a few twists of black pepper.

Carve up and serve immediately as part of a bigger spread. Roast veggies, a lovely warm kale salad, and some eggplant or chickpea dip would go beautifully with this vegetarian main.

The quickest, tastiest greens around.

SERVES 4

A friend of mine who is a fantastic chef, showed me how to cook greens this way. I love this method, as none of the nutrition and flavor is lost. All too often broccoli and other green veggies are boiled in large quantities of water, meaning that all the goodness ends up in the liquid, and not on your dinner plate. You can cook different kinds of greens this way too; cooking times may vary a little, but the method is still the same. I urge you to give it a try—you won't look back. If you want to jazz up your veggies at the end, try topping them with one of my herby butters (see page 114) or drizzle with one of my herb-infused oils (see pages 118–119).

EQUIPMENT

1 good skillet or sauté pan with a tight-fitting lid (or use a heavy-bottomed saucepan)

FOR THE VEGGIES

A few handfuls of broccolini

A handful of fine green beans, topped, but not tailed

A handful of curly kale, tough stems removed

2 tablespoons olive oil

A generous pinch of sea salt and a few twists of freshly ground black pepper

Start by putting all your veggies on a plate right next to the pan—everything needs to be set up for this recipe to work well.

Set the pan over very high heat, and leave it for a few minutes to heat up really well. If you hold your hand just above the surface, you should be able to feel the heat coming off it.

Meanwhile, pour the oil and 4 tablespoons of cold water into a cup or small bowl, and add the salt and pepper. Set it beside the veggies. Make sure the lid to the pan is right beside the vegetables and the cup of seasoned liquid.

When your pan is piping hot, quickly tip in the salty, oily water, followed by the veggies, and then at top speed, slam the lid on. The water hitting the hot surface of the pan will create a huge amount of steam, and this will cook the vegetables beautifully, while locking in all the flavor and goodness, and the oil, salt, and pepper will season it as it cooks. The salt also helps the greens retain their lovely vibrant color. You need to get the lid on super fast to catch all the steam; if you don't, the technique won't work as well as it should. Leave the veggies to cook briefly—2–3 minutes should do it. Test by carefully lifting up one side of the lid, and quickly scooping out a piece of broccolini and tasting it. You want it tender, but not soft—it's best with a little bit of a bite. When it's done, remove the lid, and using a pair of tongs, place all the veggies onto a waiting plate.

You can serve them as they are, or top with a knob of butter, or for extra flavor, use one of my flavored herby butters or oils—the wild garlic oil would be sublime.

Spiced cauliflower toasts.

SERVES 4

These delicious little toasts are a revelation. You can serve them with fried eggs, because let's face it, fried egg ain't so good without something to catch that beautiful runny yolk. You could also use them in lots of other delicious ways: topped with guacamole and a green salad, or with pan-fried mushrooms and slow-roast tomatoes. Cauliflower is wonderful in so many ways, and I for one am very thankful for the recent image overhaul that cauliflower seems to have gone through.

---

1 large cauliflower
A generous drizzle of ghee
   or olive oil
3–4 tablespoons Za'atar
   (see page 108), or
   Pistachio and Kale Ash

Dukkah (page 104), or
   just a sprinkle of ground
   cumin and paprika
Sea salt and freshly
   ground black pepper

Preheat the oven to 350°F.

Trim the base of the cauliflower so it sits flat on the board, but don't cut too much off, as you need it to hold the slices in shape.

Slice the cauliflower from top to bottom into 1¼-inch slices. Lay the slices and the ends out on a baking sheet, sprinkle with ghee or oil, then with your chosen spice mix. Season with salt and pepper.

Transfer the baking sheet to the oven and bake the toasts for about 25 minutes, or until just catching at the edges and taking on a lovely color.

Remove them from the oven, and top with anything you like. Perhaps garlicky, buttery greens (see page 48), and either a poached or fried egg (see pages 67 and 69).

Herbed cauliflower rice.

SERVES 4 AS A SIDE

This is a great little dish to make if you don't want to or can't eat grains. It goes really well with barbecued meat, or vegetarian mains in place of rice or couscous.

A handful of cashews
½ cauliflower
Juice of 1 lemon
Extra virgin olive oil
1 garlic clove, finely
   grated

A handful of fresh
   cilantro, roughly
   chopped
6 mint stalks, leaves only,
   torn
Seeds of ½ pomegranate
Sea salt and freshly
   ground black pepper

Start by dry toasting the cashews in a skillet over medium heat. Toss them every 20 seconds so they don't burn. Toast for a few minutes until they are nicely colored on all sides. Remove from the pan, and place the nuts on a board, chop roughly, then set aside.

Remove the thick inner stalk from the cauliflower. Cut it first into slices, then chop the slices into pieces the size of rice grains. (If you have a food processor you can use it to blitz the cauliflower slices, but be careful not to make the mix too fine, or it will turn into a pulp.)

When you have a chunky mix, tip it into a large bowl, squeeze over the lemon juice, add a few good glugs of olive oil, the garlic and cashews, and mix thoroughly. Add the herbs, season with salt and pepper, and sprinkle over the pomegranate seeds. Et voilà.

A simple spatchcock
chicken with a crispy skin.

SERVES 4-6

Spatchcocking a chicken is a great way of achieving a really crispy skin, which we all love.

You could keep it simple and simply spatchcock the "chook", then baste with ghee, sprinkle with salt and pepper, and roast, or you could spice it up as I have done here with my za'atar spice mix from page 108. Both kids and adults love this dish, and it's so easy to create.

The combination of za'atar spices, crispy skin and tender meat is sublime, but try cooking this with any of the Spice Mixes from pages 104–108—it will be just as delicious.

EQUIPMENT	TO SERVE
2 full-length bamboo or metal skewers	Seeds of ½ pomegranate
Strong, sharp kitchen scissors	A small bunch of fresh cilantro or arugula
1 medium free-range chicken	Garlic and herb yogurt (see page 72)
2 tablespoons ghee	
3 tablespoons za'atar spice mix (see page 108)	

Preheat the oven to 400°F.

To spatchcock a chicken, use kitchen scissors to cut down the length of the backbone of the chicken. Remove the backbone, and open the chicken out so that it lays flat with the breast facing upward, and the thighs and legs pointing outward.

Stick the skewers through the middle of the chicken so that they form a cross. This ensures the chicken remains flat while it cooks.

Place the spatchcocked chicken on a baking sheet with low sides. Rub the ghee over the chicken, sprinkle with the za'atar spice mix, then transfer the baking sheet to the oven, and roast the bird for about 20 minutes. Turn the heat down to 350°F and roast for an additional 40 minutes. You are aiming for a crispy skin, and tender meat that falls off the bone.

Remove the sheet from the oven, and allow the chicken to rest, uncovered, for about 10 minutes before serving. I like mine strewn with pomegranate seeds and cilantro or arugula leaves. Some delicious garlicky herby yogurt on the side wouldn't go amiss either.

Further seasoning and serving suggestions.
1 spatchcocked chicken cooked with Piri-piri spice mix (see page 106), served with guacamole (see page 100), and a green salad.

1 spatchcocked chicken cooked with the Mediterranean herb mix (see page 108), served with homemade fries and my garlic aioli (see page 74), or probiotic tomato ketchup (see page 86), or both and green salad on the side.

My toolbox tips for roast chicken.

Roast chicken is a meal that you can pop in the oven without too much stress or thinking. It's great for a Sunday roast, or for a weeknight supper, which can then be turned into more meals by using the leftovers. Throwing away a leftover carcass is an illegal act in my household. Even if it's just the carcass that's left, that can still be turned into another meal by making stock or bone broth as a base for a soup or risotto.

I would like to say at this point that there is no "right way" of roasting a chicken, it's really down to individual choice, and the end result you want. If you like a crisp skin, you can't add lots of liquid or wine to the roasting dish. If you want lots of juices in the pan, you have to sacrifice the crisp skin to some degree. It's nigh on impossible to have both perfect. To truss or not to truss? I don't usually bother, but if you are stuffing your chicken or want a particularly neat-looking roast bird, trussing is a good idea. You can brine the bird before you cook it for extra-tender and juicy meat, but it's certainly not an essential step to create a tender and delicious roast chicken. There are, however, a few simple rules that I have included here to help you create the perfect roast chicken that will never let you down.

For an extra-tender juicy chicken, poach the bird for 10 minutes in barely simmering water. This will give you slightly less crispy skin, but the flesh will be meltingly tender.

Allow the chicken to sit, uncovered, for several hours in the fridge before you take it out for cooking. This allows the skin to dry out, and will help you to create that lovely crisp skin.

Never put a bird in the oven straight from the fridge—always let it come up to room temperature before roasting.

Put the chicken into a roasting dish that is the right size. If there is too much room around the chicken, the juices will burn.

Always roast your chicken in a preheated oven.

If the juices in the pan are difficult to reach to spoon over the bird, baste it with melted butter.

Always allow your bird to rest before carving. It allows the meat fibers to relax, and become more tender after the cooking process, resulting in a very juicy and tender roast chicken. If you are worried you have overcooked it, turn it upside down to rest, breast-side down. This will help the juices to soak back into the dry breast.

If it's extra crispy skin you're after, roast the chicken on a rack, and cook at a higher temperature.

Buy the best bird you can afford. The health benefits of a free-range organic chicken are well-known, and the leftover carcass is perfect for making bone broth; this outweighs the extra cost of the bird by creating another meal or two.

A general time and temperature guide for roasting chicken: 20 minutes in a preheated oven at 350°F, then 15 minutes per pound.

To test if the bird is cooked, pull the thigh away from the main part of the body, and poke a sharp knife into the thickest part. If the juices run clear, the chicken is done.

Perfect roast beef.

SERVES 6-8

This is my fail-safe roast beef recipe that always ticks the boxes for a special Sunday roast. You could use topside for a casual Sunday meal, or if you really want to go to town and wow your friends and family, I would cook a sirloin roast, on the bone with the fillet still in it, or a rib of beef. I love my beef medium rare, served with a beautiful homemade creamy horseradish sauce. It is just a match made in heaven, and if you can find wild horseradish to make your sauce with, all the more wonderful.

For horseradish sauce recipes see page 80.

5-pound cut of beef—topside, sirloin, or rib (roughly 3 ribs if using a rib roast)	3–4 small red onions, halved
	1 white onion, halved
	1 whole garlic bulb, halved widthwise
1 tablespoon mustard powder (optional)	
1 tablespoon spelt flour (optional)	Salt and freshly ground black pepper

Preheat the oven to 475°F.

Ensure the beef is at room temperature, and if you are using mustard powder and flour, rub them over the layer of fat, then season generously with salt and pepper. If you are not using mustard/flour, simply season the beef with the salt and pepper.

Lay the onions and garlic in the bottom of a roasting pan, lay the beef on top and put the pan into the oven for 20 minutes. Then turn down the heat to 375°F and cook the roast for 15 minutes per pound—this will give you rare beef. Add 15 minutes to the total cooking time for medium-rare and 30 minutes to the total cooking time for well-done.

While the beef cooks, take the pan out of the oven every so often to baste the meat with its juices—simply tilt the pan and spoon the liquid over the meat. This will help keep the meat moist and succulent. Try to do this as quickly as possible, so that you don't lose heat from the oven while the door is open.

When the beef is done to your liking, remove it from the oven, and transfer it from the hot pan to a platter or board, cover loosely with foil, and a clean dishtowel, and allow to rest for at least 30 minutes.

As the meat rests it will release some juices—make sure you add those to the pan when you make the gravy.

When you have made your gravy (see instructions below), and the meat has rested, carve it, and serve alongside your favorite roast beef accompaniments.

A rough guide to making a tasty light gravy that goes beautifully with the rare roast beef... The amount of juice in the roasting pan is determined by the size of the piece of meat you cooked, which, in turn, will determine how much red wine and extra beef stock/broth you need to add. If you only roasted a small joint, and there isn't much juice, place the dish over high heat, add a splash of red wine, let it bubble quite hard for 1 minute, then add enough beef broth/stock to make as much gravy as you need. Reduce until thickened slightly, taste and season well, take off the heat, and whisk in a knob of cold butter. Pour into a pitcher or gravy boat and serve. Follow this same method for larger quantities of juice from bigger joints, tasting as you go and adding a few glugs of red wine instead of a small splash.

A perfectly juicy steak—4 ways.

SERVES 2

I have to say that rib-eye is my favorite cut of steak. For me, it has the perfect balance of juiciness and flavor; I also prefer its texture compared with other steak. Sirloin is probably my second, and fillet my third, but that's debatable. It took me a while to get the hang of cooking steak—it can be quite daunting at first, trying to get it right. The method below is pretty foolproof, and should give you a lovely, juicy steak that is well seasoned. You can keep it simple, or, for a steak with a bit of attitude, marinate it before cooking. You could also use the teriyaki sauce on page 87 for a Japanese-style steak. For an incredible flavor combination, try serving my chimichurri sauce (see page 82) with a perfectly cooked juicy steak seasoned simply with salt and pepper or with the Middle-Eastern or Mediterranean marinade below.

---

2 medium rib-eye steaks, about ¾–1-inch thick
4 tablespoons ghee or olive oil
Sea salt and freshly ground black pepper

A few marinades to choose from...
MIDDLE EASTERN
1 teaspoon sumac
1 teaspoon cumin
A few thyme sprigs
A few fresh oregano leaves
1–2 slices of orange (optional)
2 garlic cloves

MEDITERRANEAN
2 garlic cloves
2 clementines
A few thyme sprigs
A small handful of basil leaves

ASIAN-STYLE
2 teaspoons tamari
Zest and juice of 1 lime
1 teaspoon coconut sugar
2 teaspoons freshly grated ginger
½ teaspoon toasted sesame oil

Put the steak in a glass mixing bowl or non-metallic dish. Pour over the ghee or olive oil, sprinkle with salt and pepper, a generous amount—more than you might think. At this point you can keep it as is, or add the ingredients for one of the marinades. Using your hands, give it all a good mix, massaging the seasonings gently into the steak. Cover, and pop in the fridge overnight, or for up to 3 days.

When you are ready to cook the steaks, remove them from the fridge at least 1 hour before you want to cook them.

Heat a ridged grill pan until smoking hot. Place the steaks onto the smoking pan and leave them to cook for 1½–2 minutes—don't try to move them at all. Then flip them over, and cook for 1½–2 minutes on the other side. That timing will give you a rare steak; cook for an additional minute for a medium-rare to medium steak.

When the meat is cooked to your liking, remove it from the pan and place it on a plate or clean chopping board and cover loosely with foil—you don't want it to steam—and rest for at least 5–10 minutes before you eat it. Resting helps the steak to relax, soften, and become more tender. Slice into lovely thick wedges and serve.

Always ensure the steak is at room temperature before cooking it; this will allow for even cooking.

The cooking time will, of course, vary depending on how thin or thick your steak is. Cook for less time for a thinner steak, and allow more time for a thicker steak.

When the steak first hits the grill pan, respect that first contact, and don't move it. Leaving the steak alone allows it to form a nice crust and caramelize beautifully.

The perfect nutrient-dense Bolognese.

SERVES 4–6

There are almost as many versions of this controversial dish as there are Italian *nonnas* in the world. Over the years I have come up with what I think is a delicious and satisfying version, with the bonus that it is also incredibly nutrient-dense and easy to make. It's a great dish to make more than you need, and pop the rest in the freezer for a quick meal when you need something in a hurry. The liver and bone broth are the secret ingredients here for making this ragù super nutrient-dense. The addition of cacao is certainly not Italian, but it adds a depth to the flavor that is hard to put your finger on when you taste it, yet deeply delicious.

A generous knob of butter

4 ounces smoked bacon, finely diced

1 onion, finely diced

1 carrot, peeled and finely diced

2 celery stalks, finely diced

2 garlic cloves, minced

1 rosemary sprig, leaves picked and finely chopped

10 ounces coarsely ground beef, at room temperature

¼ cup chicken livers, finely chopped

⅔ cup chicken bone broth (see page 136), or quality chicken stock

Finely grated nutmeg

⅔ cup dry white wine

14 ounces tomato purée

Handful of sweet cherry tomatoes

1 teaspoon tomato paste

1 teaspoon unsweetened chocolate, finely grated (optional)

Sea salt and freshly ground black pepper

Melt the butter in a heavy-bottomed flameproof casserole dish with a tight-fitting lid over medium heat. When the butter is sizzling, add the bacon, then the onion, and cook until softened. Next add the carrot, and cook for a few minutes, then add the celery, garlic, and rosemary, and cook for a few minutes more. The vegetables should start to become meltingly tender, the onion should be softened, and the bacon will have released its fat, and be starting to smell wonderfully fragrant.

Add the ground beef to the pan, breaking it up with a wooden spoon. Brown the beef, stirring every so often to break up any lumps. Season lightly with salt and pepper to tease out the flavors, then add the liver, and allow this mix to cook for about 5 minutes.

Pour in the chicken bone broth, and grate over a little nutmeg—¼ teaspoon or less. Simmer until almost all the broth has evaporated, which should take about 30 minutes.

Pour in the wine, tomato purée, cherry tomatoes, and tomato paste, and stir well. If using chocolate, add that now too. Put the casserole dish in the oven, with the lid partially covered, and cook for at least 3½ hours until the entire mixture has really come together, and the meat is deliciously tender, fragrant, and flavorsome. Check it every so often, and top up with chicken bone broth or water if it seems too dry. If your oven runs hot, reduce the temperature a little to keep the Bolognese from drying out. Before serving, season to taste with salt and pepper.

Serve with zucchini noodles (see page 38) or even a hasselback sweet potato (see page 44) and a sprinkle of Parmesan or Pecorino cheese.

Vedge-loaded burger patties (or meatballs).

SERVES 4-6

These are my delicious vedge-loaded burger patties, a nutrient-dense version of the classic patty. You can also use this mix to make meatballs, which is actually how I came up with the idea. I was making meatballs, and experimenting with adding veggies instead of bread crumbs. The mix works great cooked both ways. The kids don't even know that you've added lots of veggies to their delicious burger! You could use carrots or beets, or grated zucchini with some of the liquid squeezed out. Here I've kept the flavoring simple, but you could add a teaspoon of one of my Spice Mixes from pages 104–108 to add a bit of attitude to the mix. Try different accompaniments, too: for example, if you add some of the Moroccan spice mix to the patties, you could serve up a green salad and some of the flavored yogurt from page 72.

4 tablespoons ghee
1 large onion, finely
  chopped
1 pound ground beef
2 large carrots, finely
  grated
1 teaspoon sea salt

½ teaspoon freshly
  ground black pepper
1 egg, lightly beaten
  (optional)
1 tablespoon finely
  chopped thyme or
  parsley (optional)

Set a large skillet over quite high heat. Add 2 tablespoons of the ghee, and fry the onion for about 5 minutes, or until golden and softened. Remove from the pan, and set aside to cool. Wipe the pan clean.

Put all the remaining ingredients, except the ghee, in a mixing bowl, add the onion, and give everything a good stir with your hands, squeezing the mixture between your fingers until it becomes sticky and fully mixed.

To make burgers, wet your hands and shape big spoonfuls of the mix into burger-shaped patties. You can make the burgers whatever size and thickness you like, but I tend to make 4–6 with this amount of mixture. To make meatballs, simply take small spoonfuls and then roll them between the palms of your hands to create walnut-sized balls.

Put the pan back on medium heat, and add the remaining ghee. When it is hot, add the patties or meatballs, and cook until nice and brown on all sides and cooked through. The time they take will vary depending on the strength of the heat, and the size you have made them, but generally, the burgers would need 3–4 minutes on each side, and meatballs might take 10 minutes in total. If they're burning on the outside before the middle is cooked, reduce the heat. The burgers can also be cooked on a grill pan or barbecue.

Serve the burgers with a salad and your favorite sauces—my probiotic tomato ketchup (see page 86) is excellent with them. You could also serve with homemade oven fries (see page 42).

If you've made meatballs, serve them as they are, or make the tomato sauce on page 84 for a good old meatball supper, served over the zucchini noodles on page 38, and topped with Parmesan cheese.

Shoulder of lamb with rose harissa and fennel.

SERVES 6-8

Cooking a shoulder of lamb couldn't be more easy than this. With a long, slow cook, the meat literally falls off the bone, and lamb, fennel, and rose harissa make for a delightful ménage à trois. This is an easy way to cook lamb shoulder, and the basic method can be used with other spice combinations. If you have any extra dried rose petals, sprinkle them over the dish at the end for a final flourish. This lamb goes beautifully with my garlicky minty yogurt on page 72.

4 large onions, halved and
    finely sliced
6 fennel bulbs, cleaned,
    trimmed, and each cut
    into 6 wedges
4 whole bulbs of garlic
Juice of ½ lemon
3½ tablespoons sherry
    vinegar
1 cup red wine
⅓ cup olive oil or ghee
2 heaping tablespoons
    rose harissa (see page
    109)
3¼ pounds shoulder of
    lamb on the bone

TO SERVE
Dried rose petals
    (optional, but they do
    add a certain fragrance
    and beauty)
Pomegranate seeds
    (optional)

Preheat the oven to 350°F.

Select a large roasting pan, big enough to hold the lamb and fennel quite snugly. Put the onions, fennel, and garlic in the pan, and pour over the lemon juice, vinegar, wine, and olive oil. Next rub the rose harissa over the top of the shoulder of lamb, massaging it in gently. Nestle the shoulder into the vegetables, and then pour over 5 cups of cold water. Cover the whole dish in a double layer of foil, ensuring there are no gaps.

Transfer the pan to the oven, and cook for 1 hour, then reduce the temperature to 300°F, and cook for an additional 4–5 hours, or until the meat is meltingly tender, and falls off the bone at the prod of a fork. For the final 30 minutes, remove the foil, and increase the heat to 325°F. When the lamb is done, carefully transfer it to a serving platter.

Strain and discard the fat from the vegetables. The slow-cooked onions and fennel should now resemble a tender vegetable chutney. Serve the slow-cooked fennel compote with the lamb, and sprinkle over some dried rose petals if you have some. If you like, you could also scatter over some pomegranate seeds for added color, and a pop of freshness and acidity.

Don't carve the meat; instead use two forks to pull it off the bone.

Try serving with flavored yogurt (see page 72), a big green salad with pomegranate seeds (see page 20), or herbed cauliflower rice (see page 49).

A crispy skin fillet of fish.

SERVES 1

My son loves crispy skin on his fish, so I have perfected the art of achieving it. This is a super-easy, no-fuss way of cooking fish—great for a quick and healthy midweek meal. Fish is full of anti-inflammatory omega 3s, brain-boosting healthy fats, and vitamin D, which every single metabolic process in the body requires—and it just happens to be delicious!

Fish fillet cooked this way is great as it is, served with a lovely crisp green salad, or, for a truly comforting and hearty meal, serve it with my probiotic tomato ketchup (see page 86) and homemade oven (see page 42).

---

1 fillet of fish (about 8 ounces), skin on (salmon, sea bass, pollock, cod, snapper, hake, or red mullet are good choices)

Ghee or grapeseed oil (or you could use olive oil or cold-pressed sunflower oil)
A knob of butter (optional)
½ lemon
Sea salt and freshly ground black pepper

Get the pan really hot over medium–high heat—leave it for several minutes before you start cooking. I use a heavy-bottomed steel or cast-iron pan. A nonstick pan prevents sticking, but you won't get the skin really brown and golden.

First wash the fillet, then dry it really well with paper towels, otherwise the skin won't crisp. Season on both sides with salt and black pepper.

When the pan is hot, and the fish is seasoned, coat the pan with a little oil—enough to give an even coating on the pan. Use one with a high smoke point like ghee or grapeseed. Allow the oil to heat, and just before it starts to smoke, quickly add the fish, skin-side down.

The fillet will contract and curve upwards. When this happens, take a flexible spatula and press the entire fillet gently back down, and hold for a few seconds. This will ensure even cooking and crispy skin all over.

Leave the fish to cook, without messing with it too much. When you can see a lovely golden brown color on the edge of the skin, and the edges of the fish flesh become opaque, carefully and gently use a spatula to lift up the fillet and flip it over. The fish is delicate, so try not to break it up. At this point it's already about three-quarters cooked, so it will need only another couple of minutes on the second side.

Add a knob of butter for flavor at this point if you like, and use it to baste the fish while it finishes cooking.

Remove from the pan, and serve with a squeeze of lemon and your favorite sides.

Eggs, glorious eggs.

I am so happy that medical science has finally caught up with common sense in recent years with regard to the humble egg. The delicious little orb of goodness has been given a bad name in the past few decades, with scientists telling us that eating eggs raises our cholesterol levels. Happily, this myth has been thoroughly debunked, so we can all go back to having eggs for breakfast, guilt-free. Although, I'll freely admit, I've never not had eggs for breakfast at least a couple of times a week. They're my go-to quick and nutritious fast food. Almost nothing on earth is as delicious as a soft-boiled egg, with a tiny knob of butter and salt and pepper, sprinkled into the hole in the top—absolute heaven. I love eggs all ways: softly scrambled, gently poached, fried in ghee, cooked as a Spanish tortilla, or with vegetables in a frittata, as a soft-centered omelet... Middle-Eastern shakshuka eggs are amazing too. There are endless ways you can serve an egg.

Eggs are one of the most nutritious foods on the planet, an original superfood. They are loaded with vitamins A, B_2, B_5, B_{12}, folate, phosphorus, and selenium. Eggs also provide vitamins D, E, K, B_6, calcium, and zinc, and they're packed with protein and healthy fats. To get all this nutritional benefit, you must eat them as a whole food, though; don't eat just the whites, or just the yolks.

When buying eggs, it's very important to remember that quality is paramount. Barn-raised hens that have no access to sunlight and don't have a healthy diet, do not lay healthy eggs. Eggs laid by these deprived birds just don't have anywhere near the same levels of immune-boosting, brain-boosting goodness they should contain. So please try to buy organic, free-range eggs from birds that are free to enjoy grass, bugs, and sunlight, all the things chickens need to lay healthy, delicious, and nutritious eggs. Better still, buy some hens and have your own fresh eggs every morning!

Softly softly scrambled eggs.

SERVES 2

Soft scrambled eggs have to be one of the most comforting foods. If you want to make the following recipe dairy-free, omit the cream (although it does make for a very soft, creamy scramble) and cook the eggs using ghee or coconut oil instead of butter.

4 organic, free-range eggs	Small handful of parsley or chervil, or both
Dash of cream (optional)	Sea salt and freshly ground black pepper
A knob of butter (or ghee or coconut oil)	

Set a medium skillet over medium heat on the smallest ring of your stovetop.

Crack the eggs into a bowl, and whisk briskly with a fork. You don't need the yolks and whites to completely emulsify; it's nice if they are still a little separate. Add the cream, if using, and season with salt and pepper.

Add the butter to the pan, and let it sizzle a little. Pour the egg mix into the pan, and turn the heat down to low.

Gently stir using a wooden spoon, carefully turning the eggs so the bottom layer gets lifted to the top and the top is turned to the bottom to scramble the eggs evenly. They will take 4–5 minutes to cook. Don't rush it: slow and gentle is key here.

When the eggs are mostly scrambled but still have a luscious creaminess to them, sprinkle over the herbs, and then plate up. Best eaten with fresh sourdough bread or other homemade bread.

These eggs are good served with my slow-roasted tomatoes from page 43, and a sprinkle of dukkah (see page 104).

A delicious fried egg, with crispy sage.

SERVES 1–2

Cooking eggs this way makes them perfect for topping noodle dishes, fried greens, roasted sweet potatoes or pretty much anything. I like the way they puff up and go really crispy. If you want to create the classic fried egg, just use less oil—about half a tablespoon.

2–3 tablespoons ghee or odorless coconut oil	6–8 sage leaves
2 eggs	Sea salt and freshly ground black pepper

Put a medium or small pan over quite high heat. When it starts to warm up, add the ghee or coconut oil, and allow the oil to warm—you don't want it smoking, though, just hot enough for the egg to sizzle, but not explode. Crack the eggs straight into the pan, keeping them at quite a high temperature, so that the edges go crispy. As the eggs cook, tilt the pan and spoon over the hot fat.

When the edges are crisp, and no parts of the white are still runny or uncooked, use a fish slice or slotted spoon to slide the eggs out of the pan and onto a waiting dish.

Once you've scooped out the eggs, throw in the sage leaves and cook for no more than 15–20 seconds. Scoop them out and sprinkle over the fried eggs along with some sea salt and black pepper.

Serve over freshly cooked noodle or rice dishes, toasted sourdough bread with avocado, or slow-roasted tomatoes, or with roasted veggies and a green salad.

If teaching kids to fry an egg, add only a little oil to the pan, and show them how to crack the egg into a teacup first, which makes it quicker and safer for little hands to pour the egg into the pan holding the cup handle, rather than cracking the egg directly into the hot fat, which can spit.

SAVORY PANTRY Salads Vegetables and Sides Meat and Fish *Eggs* Flavored Yogurts Mayonnaise Sauces Salsa and Chutneys

A perfect poached egg.

SERVES 1

Many people have asked me how to create the perfect poached egg, and to my mind, it's all down to the freshness of the egg. Unfortunately, finding very fresh eggs is not always possible. Supermarket eggs are not actually that fresh. Even though they are well within their use-by date, this doesn't mean they were laid the day before. If you crack an egg that has just been laid, the white of the egg will hold its shape, nice and neat, not spread out. If you crack open an egg that is more than a few days old—even a week or two old—the white will spread right out, covering a large area.

When you are poaching an egg, a super-fresh one will hold that lovely neat shape beautifully, creating the perfect poached beauty. Poaching an egg that is anything less than super fresh will have that craggy look, very untidy, and not at all the lovely thing we are after. I might add, though, that they will both taste wonderful, it's just that they don't look the same. However, there are a few tricks that will help you to create the perfect-looking poached egg even when it is not a super-fresh one.

1–2 organic, free-range eggs per person, as fresh as you can find

2 teaspoons apple cider vinegar (this helps the eggs to hold their shape)

Fill a medium, high-sided skillet with water to a depth of a couple of inches, set over medium heat, and bring to a bare simmer—you don't want the water to boil.

Crack your first egg into a ramekin or teacup, and have your toast or salad ready before you start to cook.

Add the vinegar to the pan of barely simmering water, then carefully swirl the water to make a gentle whirlpool. Slide the egg carefully, white first, into the center of the whirlpool. Allow the egg to cook a little then move it out of the center with a slotted spoon, then repeat with a second egg.

The eggs only take about 2–3 minutes to cook for a soft poached yolk. You can lift them up out of the water with the slotted spoon and give the yolks a prod to see how done they are. If they are ready, lay them onto paper towels to drain or, if they need more cooking, lower them gently back into the water to cook a little longer.

Once the eggs are cooked and drained, transfer them to your waiting toast or salad, and serve immediately to ensure they are lovely and hot when you eat them.

If you are making lots of poached eggs, use two pans of barely simmering water. Make the first pan your whirlpool pan, then transfer the eggs to the second pan to finish their cooking. You can cook several eggs more quickly this way.

If you only have one pan, don't use the whirlpool method; just place the eggs around the edge of the pan in a circle. You may not get such tidy results, but the eggs will still be delicious—you can always trim the whites with scissors if necessary after they have finished cooking to create tidy shapes.

The perfectly luscious green cheesy omelet.

SERVES 1

Simple, cheap, nutritious and delicious, an omelet can be ready in under a minute, which will demand from the cook quick wits and a keen eye. You can add endless things: crispy bacon, fried mushrooms, smoked salmon, and red onion are all wonderful options. There are different kinds of omelets, too. The easiest to create at home is the English half moon. Be patient, and over time you will become an omelet master.

---

2 free-range eggs
A small handful of very finely chopped parsley leaves
A generous knob of butter

A small handful of grated Cheddar cheese
Sea salt and freshly ground black pepper

Crack the eggs into a bowl. Add the parsley, and using a metal whisk or fork, give the eggs a quick whisk, until just mixed, then season lightly.

Warm a skillet over medium heat. Add the butter, let it foam, then swirl to coat the base of the pan. When the foam dies down a little, carefully pour in the eggs. They should gently sizzle.

Give the pan a gentle shake to distribute the eggs evenly. Using a wooden spoon or fork, pull in the sides and tilt the pan to fill in the gaps. You can do this for about the first 20 seconds, then you need to leave it to cook. After 30 seconds, add a sprinkle of cheese. When the edges have turned opaque, but the middle is still slightly runny, carefully flip half the omelet onto the other side, creating a half moon. Slide the omelet onto a waiting plate.

Add another sprinkle of salt and freshly ground pepper if you like, or an extra few parsley leaves sprinkled over the top. Eat piping hot, just as it is or with my charred cherry tomato and chili salsa (see page 92) and magical golden kraut (see page 145) for a nutrient-dense breakfast or evening meal.

Shakshuka eggs.

SERVES 4 GENEROUSLY

These delightfully soft-centered eggs braised in rich tomato sauce are the perfect treat for a special Sunday morning, or a quick week-night dinner. They are comforting, easy to prepare, and a real crowd-pleaser. I love them served with sourdough toast and fresh guacamole (see page 100) or cauliflower toasts (see page 49.)

---

1 teaspoon cumin seeds
⅔ cup ghee or olive oil
2 large onions, halved and sliced into thin half moons
2 red bell peppers, cut into strips
4 teaspoons coconut sugar or maple syrup
2 bay leaves
A few thyme sprigs, leaves only

A small handful of flat-leaf parsley, chopped
4 large ripe tomatoes, roughly chopped
14-ounce can chopped tomatoes
A pinch of saffron threads
A pinch of cayenne pepper
5–6 free-range eggs
Sea salt and freshly ground black pepper
Fresh cilantro, to serve

Place a large skillet over quite high heat and dry fry the cumin seeds for 1–2 minutes. Add the ghee and onion, and sauté for 5 minutes. Add the red peppers, coconut sugar, and herbs. Continue cooking for 5–10 minutes, or until the onions are nicely colored. Add the tomatoes, saffron, and cayenne pepper. Add a little salt and black pepper to tease out the flavors. Reduce the heat to low, and simmer gently for 15 minutes. As it cooks, keep adding a little water so that the mix is pasta-sauce consistency. Taste and adjust the seasoning. It should be flavorsome and heady.

Remove the bay leaves, then use the back of a spoon to make 5 or 6 holes in the tomato mix. Crack an egg into each hole, sprinkle with salt, and cover the pan. Cook very gently for 6–7 minutes, or until the eggs are just set, but the yolks are still runny. Remove from the heat, sprinkle with cilantro and black pepper, and serve.

Flavored yogurts.

MAKES 9 OUNCES (SERVES 4-6)

Flavored yogurts are delicious in combination with dishes that have my toolbox Spice Mixes as their flavor foundation—especially those with more Middle-Eastern and North African flavor combinations. Serving spiced roasted vegetables or meat with a generous spoonful of one of these yogurts greatly softens earthy, pungent spices.

Thick Greek-style yogurt is the best sort to use. It has a perfect consistency that provides a certain indulgent quality. It also holds additional flavors much more effectively than thinner, lighter styles. You can thicken natural yogurt by hanging it in cheesecloth over a bowl for an hour or so, allowing the whey to slowly drip out. Over time, the yogurt left in the cheesecloth will be closer to Greek yogurt in texture. There's no need to throw out the whey; add it to soups or dahl for a protein boost.

---

9 ounces thick Greek-style yogurt
1 teaspoon Tabasco or my chili sauce on page 77
Zest and juice of 1 lime
10 mint leaves, finely chopped

A good pinch of sea salt and a few twists of freshly ground black pepper
1 tablespoon extra virgin olive oil
1 garlic clove, finely grated (optional)

Mix all the ingredients in a bowl, beating well to bring the flavors together. Taste, and adjust the seasoning as necessary, adding more salt or black pepper if it needs it, or more lime juice to balance the flavors.

Cover and place the bowl in the fridge until you are ready to use it. It is greatly improved if it's given an hour or so to let the flavors come together before using. Kept sealed, it will last several days in the fridge.

Serve on top of roasted veggies or meat, or in a bowl alongside a summer barbecue spread. I think it tastes best when lightly chilled.

For a chili kick: Add 1-2 fresh medium chiles, seeds removed, and minced.
For a gingery note: Add 1 teaspoon of finely grated fresh ginger root, plus the juice.
For a full flavor bomb: Add 2 tablespoons of finely chopped cilantro, 1 finely minced garlic clove, and 1 fresh medium chile, seeds removed and finely chopped.

My classic mayonnaise base.

MAKES 2½ CUPS

Mayonnaise bases work by rounding out and completing a dish, adding a certain complexity to the final flavor. A variety of ingredients can be added to the base, making it compatible with what you are cooking, including saffron, garlic, roasted nuts, green herbs, anchovies, lemon zest, kimchi, and sriracha. These mayonnaise bases work particularly well with Mediterranean flavors, except for the kimchi and sriracha variations, which, unsurprisingly, work well with Asian-inspired flavors.

I tend to use extra virgin olive oil as the only oil in my mayonnaise, but some people find that too intense. If you prefer, use half olive oil and half cold-pressed sunflower oil. If you are using solely olive oil, try to use one that is sweet and fruity, rather than green and grassy. This will give the finished mayo a much smoother flavor with no hint of bitterness.

The classic mayonnaise, with only the addition of lemon juice and zest, works beautifully with crab, white fish, shellfish, and all of the glorious summer vegetables such as asparagus, peas, and fava beans. After years cooking in a kitchen with no food processor, I still prefer to make my mayonnaise by hand; old habits die hard. However, you can just as easily use a food processor and follow the same steps. Since mayonnaise contains raw eggs, you should only make what you need for immediate use. If you want to make less than the amount here, halve the other ingredients and just use one large egg yolk.

3 organic free-range egg yolks
Juice and zest of ½ lemon
2 teaspoons Dijon mustard
2 cups mild and fruity olive oil, or 50:50 cold-pressed olive and sunflower oils
Sea salt and freshly ground black pepper

Place the egg yolks in a heavy mixing bowl (so that it won't move about while you whisk). Add the lemon juice, mustard, a good pinch of salt, and a few grinds of pepper. Whisk briefly to combine.

As you whisk, very slowly start to drizzle in the olive oil, adding just a few drops to start with. Whisk to incorporate the oil, then slowly start pouring again, whisking constantly. As you incorporate more of the oil, you can add a larger quantity at a time.

Continue to whisk and pour until all the oil has been thoroughly incorporated, and the mayonnaise is fully emulsified. If your bowl moves around too much as you whisk, place a damp cloth underneath it to reduce movement.

Taste and add extra lemon juice, salt or black pepper to your liking. Keep in the fridge until needed.

Tip: If the mayonnaise starts to split, you can usually bring it back together by adding 1 tablespoon of warm water, then continue adding the rest of the oil.

Mayonnaise (continued).

Saffron mayonnaise.
The saffron flavor works well with fish, chicken, beans, and lamb.

Infuse 15–20 strands of saffron in 1–2 tablespoons of hot water for 10 minutes, then add the saffron and infused liquid to the base mayonnaise ingredients at the very beginning.

Green herb mayonnaise.
The green notes work well with fish, chicken, greens, beans, and asparagus.

At the very beginning, mix in 2 tablespoons of finely chopped basil and parsley with the mustard and lemon juice.

Aioli.
Garlicky aioli works well with bread, chicken, lamb, fish, and beans.

Add 2 finely chopped or mashed garlic cloves at the very beginning with the mustard and lemon juice.

Anchovy mayonnaise.
The kick of anchovy goes well with fish, winter greens, chicken, and lamb.

Add 3 finely chopped or mashed anchovy fillets at the very beginning with the mustard and lemon juice.

Nutty mayonnaise.
Nutty notes go beautifully with winter veggies, chicken, fish, and lamb.

Add a small handful of roasted and finely ground nuts such as almonds, walnuts, pecans, or brazil nuts at the very beginning with the mustard and lemon juice.

Spicy rose harissa mayonnaise.
This combo is stunning with lamb, chicken, and winter squash.

Add 1 talespoon of rose harissa (see page 109) at the very beginning with the mustard and lemon juice.

Zingy kimchi mayonnaise.
This mayo goes amazingly well with fried fish.

Add 2 tablespoons of finely chopped kimchi at the very end, and mix through.

Sriracha flavor bomb.
This mayo goes well with chicken, hearty winter veggies, and pork.

Use 1 lime in place of the lemon, and add 1 tablespoon of Sriracha (see page 77) at the very end and fold through.

Fermented mayo.
Use this in place of normal mayo in any dish that you fancy. It will give you a probiotic boost, and the flavor has extra zing.

Make the classic mayo mix, add 1 tablespoon of kefir whey or yogurt whey, and mix thoroughly into the mayo. Transfer to a glass jar with a tight-fitting lid, leave on the worktop to ferment for 7–8 hours, then refrigerate. Eat within a few days.

SAVORY PANTRY Salads Vegetables and Sides Meat and Fish Eggs Flavored Yogurts Mayonnaise *Sauces* Salsa and Chutneys

Sriracha.

Rather like kimchi, this hot chili sauce is one of those magic ingredients that, once tasted, you'll add to everything. Try it with fish or roast veggies, add it to mayo, which is delicious with oven-roasted sweet potato wedges, or serve with eggs, burgers, Asian stir-fries, bowls of pho... the list is endless. Traditionally, sriracha is fermented; this is my quick version.

EQUIPMENT
Sterilized glass jars or
   bottles (see page 79)

5 ounces garlic cloves,
   peeled (about 3 bulbs)
1 pound red or green
   jalapeño chiles, seeded,
   stemmed, and ribbed,
   sliced into thin rings

2 cups apple cider vinegar
Scant ½ cup clear honey
2 tablespoons coarse sea
   salt
2 tablespoons tomato
   paste
1 tablespoon arrowroot
   (optional)
2 tablespoons fish sauce

Begin by blanching the garlic cloves: place the cloves in a small pan, cover with boiling water, and set over high heat for 30 seconds, then drain and rinse under cold water. Repeat the process.

Roughly chop the garlic, and combine with the jalapeños and vinegar in a large pan. Bring to a boil, and simmer for 3 minutes. Remove from the heat, and add the honey and salt. Stir, then set aside for a couple of hours to allow the flavors to develop.

Using a stick blender, blitz everything until completely smooth. Add the tomato paste, place back over high heat, and bring to a boil, then reduce the heat and simmer for 15–20 minutes. For a thicker sauce, dissolve the arrowroot with 1 tablespoon of lukewarm water, whisk into the simmering sauce, and cook for an additional 2 minutes. By now the sauce should have thickened.

Remove from the heat and let cool slightly, then add the fish sauce. Transfer into the jars or bottles. It keeps in the fridge for at least six months—if you can resist it for that long.

Cucumber raita.

This cooling and creamy raita is great with any kind of dahl or curry, or even alongside delicious roast meats that have a spicy base seasoning. It's an ideal accompaniment to hot dishes as the cucumber and yogurt act as coolants against the spicy heat.

1 small cucumber, peeled,
   seeded, and finely
   chopped
   or coarsely grated
Zest and juice of ½ lemon
1 cup plain full-fat yogurt
   (Greek yogurt also
   works well)

2 tablespoons finely
   chopped cilantro, plus
   a few leaves for serving
1 teaspoon lightly toasted,
   crushed cumin seeds
Sea salt and freshly
   ground black pepper

Put everything in a bowl and combine. Taste, and adjust the seasoning if it needs it, either by adding a little more lemon, or salt and black pepper. Transfer to the fridge until ready to use. This will keep well for a couple of days, but is best eaten fresh.

Try this served with my celeriac Mung Dahl (see page 33).

Finding fresh red jalapeños can be a bit tricky. Using green jalapeños is fine, but the result will be a slightly different color than the more common red sriracha. Otherwise, if you can find them, the dried jalapeño chiles sold in Asian supermarkets work really well—just be sure to soak them first to plump them up.

Plum ketchup.

This is the sauce I grew up on—my mom's famous plum ketchup. I LOVE it! If I had to choose five favorite tastes from my childhood, this would be one of them. We had it on everything from fish and chips through to shepherd's pie, or with our delicious homemade sausages. My mom always had the shelves stocked with this sauce, which we had instead of tomato ketchup. It still gives that tangy ketchup hit, but with a plum twist. This recipe makes quite a lot, which is great if you have a glut of plums, but if you don't have a plentiful supply, just halve the recipe. My mom always made large batches of this sauce to last us all the way to the next plum season.

EQUIPMENT
Sterilized wide-mouth glass bottles or jars (see below) with sealing lids or tops

7¾ pounds dark red tart plums, halved and pitted

5⅔ cups unrefined cane or coconut sugar
2⅓ cups light clear honey
2 teaspoons sea salt
1 teaspoon allspice berries
1 teaspoon whole cloves
⅓ cup grated fresh ginger
2 quarts + ½ cup cider vinegar

Put everything in a large heavy-bottomed pan, bring to a boil and simmer for 2 hours. Set aside to cool slightly. When the sauce has cooled a little, but is still hot, pour it into the bottles. Put the lids on and process in a boiling-water bath according to the jar manufacturer's instructions. Properly sealed, this ketchup will keep well for months.

Sterilizing glass jars
To sterilize glass jars, either put them through the dishwasher or boil them in a pan of boiling water for 10 minutes. Wash the lids well in warm water, rinse, then let soak in very hot water for 10 minutes.

Barbecue sauce.

Where there is bacon there must be barbecue sauce, right? Right! This sauce is also a great marinade for meat that will be barbecued, roasted, or broiled. It goes particularly well with pork, lamb, and beef.

EQUIPMENT
Sterilized glass jars with airtight lids (see below)

2¼ pounds vine-ripened tomatoes
2 tablespoons olive oil or ghee
2 red onions, minced
5 garlic cloves, crushed
1½ teaspoons smoked paprika

2½ teaspoons ground cumin
1 teaspoon brown mustard seeds
1 tablespoon thyme leaves
2 tablespoons cider vinegar
generous ⅓ cup maple syrup
2 teaspoons tamari (traditionally brewed Japanese soy sauce)
1 teaspoon Dijon mustard

Cut a cross in the base of each tomato. Put the tomatoes in a large bowl, and pour over enough boiling water to cover them. Allow the tomatoes to sit fully submerged in the water for about 1 minute. Drain and rinse well under cold water. Carefully peel away the skins, cut into quarters, and discard the skins and seeds. Roughly chop the flesh and set aside.

Heat the oil or ghee in a large saucepan over medium heat. Cook the onions, stirring occasionally, for 5 minutes, or until softened. Add the garlic, spices, and thyme, and cook, stirring, for 1 minute.

Add the tomatoes, and bring to a boil. Reduce the heat and simmer for 10–12 minutes. Add the remaining ingredients and simmer for an additional 15 minutes, or until lovely and thick.

When the sauce is ready, remove it from the heat and transfer to the jars. Secure the lids, then turn the jars upside down to seal. Allow them to cool in this position, then transfer to the fridge where they will keep very happily for at least a few weeks.

Horseradish sauce—2 ways.

SERVES 4–6

Like most things, homemade horseradish sauce is far nicer than bought versions. Using crème fraîche gives it a superior texture as well as a richness that store-bought ones lack. The lemon juice sharpens the flavor, and stops the grated horseradish from discoloring. What's more, it's SO easy and keeps in the fridge for at least 4–5 days. I like to serve this sauce both plain, and the pimped-up version with hot rare roast beef, on cold roast beef sandwiches and with a beet salad.

Unfortunately, fresh horseradish is only available for a short period each year, so grab it while you can! When making this sauce, use a spatula and fold the ingredients together lightly rather than beating or mixing. Treat the crème fraîche gently, and it will be kind back to you.

BASIC HORSERADISH SAUCE
1 cup crème fraîche (or sour cream)
1 heaping teaspoon Dijon mustard
A squeeze of lemon

2–2½-inch piece of horseradish, freshly peeled and grated (you can use more or less, depending on how strong you like it. I like mine to pack a punch)
Sea salt and freshly ground black pepper

Gently fold the ingredients together in a bowl. If you beat or mix the crème fraîche, it will collapse, and you'll end up with a runny sauce rather than a thick one. Taste and adjust the seasoning. Keep chilled until ready to use. This will keep in the fridge for several days.

Arugula horseradish sauce (the pimped-up version).
As above, but fold through a handful or two of very finely chopped arugula. Leave to sit in the fridge for 30 minutes before using.

A rosy-hued festive apple and cranberry sauce.

SERVES 8–10

This sauce sits somewhere between an applesauce and cranberry sauce, so it's more versatile than a straight-up cranberry sauce, and suitable for lots of dishes throughout the autumn and winter. It goes beautifully with any roast bird, and sits alongside all the winter veggies in perfect matrimony.

---

12 ounces cranberries (frozen work well, and there is no prepping to do)
2 sweet-tart apples, such as Granny Smith or Golden Delicious, cored and chopped into ½-inch chunks

Zest and juice of 2 clementines
⅓ cup light clear honey
1 tablespoon peeled and finely grated ginger
A pinch of ground cloves

Put all the ingredients into a medium saucepan along with scant ½ cup of water. Bring to a boil, then lower the heat and simmer for 10–15 minutes.

Remove from the heat and allow to cool a little before serving, or transfer to a glass jar with a lid. This sauce will keep in the fridge for one week.

A classic applesauce for any occasion.

This applesauce is an essential accompaniment to roast pork or pork chops. You could sweeten it further, and add a dollop to your oatmeal or granola during the colder months when apples are in abundance. However you serve it, hot or cold, it's delicious. You can use different varieties of apples to vary the flavor—heritage apples from farmers' markets lend themselves to this beautifully.

a fork to help them along. The sugars in the apples can easily catch and burn, so keep a close eye on them.

Once soft, remove from the heat and beat in the butter and sweetener. Serve at once, or transfer to a glass jar with a lid, allow to cool, and pop in the fridge. It will keep for about one week.

---

8 ounces cooking apples, such as Golden Delicious or Granny Smith, peeled, cored, and chopped Zest of ½ lemon	1½ tablespoons butter 1 tablespoon light honey, maple syrup, coconut sugar or unrefined cane sugar (or more or less to taste)

Put the apples into a saucepan with the lemon zest and 2 tablespoons of water. Cover and cook over low heat for about 10 minutes, or until the apples are soft and mushy, and completely broken down. Depending on the type of apples you have used, you may need to mash them with

If you use eating apples, you won't need as much sweetener, so make sure you taste the sauce before adding your chosen sweetener.

Chimichurri green sauce.

SERVES 4-6

Chimichurri is an Argentinian green sauce that is traditionally used on grilled, broiled, and barbecued meats and vegetables. It's seriously good, and takes only a few minutes to make. You can chill it in the fridge to create a kind of flavored oil, or just use it immediately as a topping for steaks and other broiled or grilled delights. If you like your steak Gaucho-style, this magic little green sauce is just for you.

There are as many variations of this sauce as there are grandmothers in Argentina, but they usually center around the same base components. If you like your chimichurri spicier, up the chili. You can use fresh thyme leaves if you don't have oregano.

2 small bunches of flat-leaf parsley, chopped
1 teaspoon chopped oregano—fresh is best
4 fat garlic cloves, minced
2 shallots, finely chopped
1 teaspoon red pepper flakes

7 tablespoons extra virgin olive oil
Juice of 1 lemon
4 tablespoons red wine vinegar
Sea salt and freshly ground black pepper

The best way to make this heavenly green sauce is by chopping the herbs quite finely with a very sharp knife—this way the leaves are not bruised. Transfer the herbs, garlic and shallots to a small bowl and stir in the rest of the ingredients. Taste and adjust the seasoning as necessary. Eat within a few days.

Alternatively, if you are pushed for time or don't have a really good sharp knife, you can put everything into a food processor and blitz until you have a chunky sauce—not too fine but not too rough; somewhere in the middle is perfect. Spoon into a bowl and chill until ready to use.

Greener than green mint sauce (Grandma's special recipe).

SERVES 4-6

This is my Grandma Maida's special recipe; she served up the best mint sauce I know, and just thinking about it I can recall the piquant tang and delightful sweetness of her sauce right now. Admittedly, I have swapped the more traditional form of sweetener (white sugar) for a less refined one. Coconut sugar has a much lower level of fructose and doesn't cause the same spike in blood-sugar levels. I'm sure you'll love this stuff as much as I do. Next time you roast a leg of spring lamb, don't forget this great sauce on the side.

A medium bunch of mint
A pinch of sea salt
1 rounded tablespoon
 coconut sugar or
 unrefined cane sugar
⅓ cup boiling water
⅓ cup raw cider vinegar

Wash the mint thoroughly under running water, then drain and spin in a salad spinner to remove excess moisture. Strip the mint leaves off their stalks (discard the stalks or make tea from them to sip while you make your sauce!).

Sprinkle the leaves with a pinch of salt, then finely chop them. Put them in a pitcher, add the coconut sugar and pour over the boiling water, stir, and leave to cool. Stir in the vinegar, and adjust the seasoning to your taste.

Serve with roasted, broiled, or barbecued lamb.

A creamy cheese sauce (and a cauliflower and cheese).

MAKES 3½ CUPS

This is my go-to cheese sauce for making cauliflower and cheese, or a smoked fish pie. It's rich, creamy, and decadent, but with a little kick from the nutmeg and cayenne, both welcome additions. You could use the sauce as a luxurious warm dip for steamed veggies or for lasagna, using thick zucchini ribbons instead of pasta for a gluten-free supper dish.

---

2 tablespoons unsalted
 butter
⅓ cup white spelt flour
2¾ cups whole milk
A good pinch of sea salt
A good pinch of ground
 white pepper
A pinch of cayenne
 pepper
A pinch of grated nutmeg
¾ cup cheese, grated
 (Cheddar, Gouda, or
 Gruyère)
*If making a fish pie,
 add 2-3 tablespoons
 finely chopped parsley,
 1-2 teaspoons Dijon
 mustard and a good
 squeeze of lemon juice

Melt the butter in a saucepan over medium heat. Stir in the flour and cook for 2-3 minutes, mixing well with a spoon or whisk. Remove from the heat, and gradually add the milk, whisking between additions to get rid of lumps, to make a smooth sauce.

Return to the heat and bring to a boil, stirring. Simmer gently for 8-10 minutes. Stir in the salt, white pepper, nutmeg, and cayenne. If the sauce is destined for a fish pie, add the parsley, mustard, and lemon juice. Sprinkle in the cheese and allow it to melt—don't re-boil, or the cheese will become stringy. It is now ready to use.

To make cauliflower and cheese, simply steam the florets of a cauliflower for 5 minutes until tender but not too soft. Transfer to a medium baking dish, pour over the cheese sauce and sprinkle with a little extra cayenne or sourdough breadcrumbs, then roast at 350°F for 15-20 minutes until golden. Flash under the broiler at the end if needed, to get that golden bubbling deliciousness. Serves 6.

My favorite tomato sauce
for pasta, zucchini noodles, and beans.

SERVES 3-4

This is my alternative to tomato sauce that has been made from a can. I am not a fan of the way sauce made with canned tomatoes turns out, although they can be handy when you are in a pinch. If I have fresh tomatoes on hand, though, I much prefer this lighter, fresher version.

I use a variety of red, orange, and yellow tomatoes mixed in with the classic red cherry ones. Apart from their visual impact, yellow and orange tomatoes contain increased amounts of lycopene, the coloring pigment in tomatoes that is known to have important anti-cancer properties.

---

10 ounces cherry tomatoes, or a mix of red, orange, and yellow cherry and plum tomatoes

4–6 garlic cloves, peeled and lightly bashed

A few basil leaves, plus extra for serving

scant ½ cup olive oil

Sea salt and freshly ground black pepper

Simply put everything in a smallish saucepan over medium–high heat and cover with a lid. When it's really bubbling, turn the heat down to medium. Keep the lid on and simmer quite vigorously for about 20 minutes. The tomatoes will break down and release all their juices and everything will be quite well incorporated.

I like this sauce quite chunky, but you can mash the tomatoes with a fork to break it down further if you like.

For a warming, filling meal, spoon over your favorite pasta, spiralized zucchini, or even cooked cranberry beans, and sprinkle with shaved Parmesan and plenty of torn basil leaves.

Try adding a pinch of red pepper flakes, or replacing the basil with rosemary (especially if you are planning to serve it with slow-cooked cranberry beans).

Probiotic tomato ketchup.

MAKES 4¼ CUPS

This stuff is amazing: piquant, tangy, sweet, and addictive all at once. I make this for my son because he loves to smother his homemade fries in sauce, and indeed many other things too. I don't have to worry that he's piling on too much, because I know it's super-healthy: it's packed full of immune-boosting probiotics that support gut health, digestion, brain function, and much more. As the sauce ferments, the bacteria eat the sugars it contains, so by the time it's ready for your plate, it's practically sugar free—another bonus. The longer the ketchup ferments, the more sour it becomes. After it's been in the fridge for over a month, the flavor can be really tangy—almost fizzy—which I like, but for serving it to the kids, you can just add a little more sweetener, and it's good to go.

EQUIPMENT
Sterilized glass jar with a
  lid large enough to hold
  about 34 fluid ounces
  (see page 79)
A funnel

2 tablespoons ghee or
  butter
2 medium onions, roughly
  chopped
2 shallots, roughly
  chopped
2 garlic cloves, roughly
  chopped
2 bay leaves
7 tablespoons cider
  vinegar
28 ounces tomato sauce
7 tablespoons maple
  syrup or light clear
  honey

½ teaspoon ground cumin
A pinch of cayenne
  pepper
Sea salt and freshly
  ground black pepper

FOR THE FERMENT STARTER
2 tablespoons of
  sauerkraut juice or
  fermented pickle juice
  from any of the wild
  fermented pickles
  recipes (see pages
  145–153), or whey from
  either dairy yogurt or
  milk kefir

Put a medium saucepan or high-sided skillet with a lid over medium heat and add the ghee. Then add the onions, shallots, garlic, and bay leaves, and give them a good stir. When they are sizzling, reduce the heat, and allow everything to caramelize for 10 minutes, or until softened and turned a lovely golden color.

Turn up the heat and pour in the vinegar, allowing it to evaporate a little. Add the rest of the ingredients, and then reduce the heat again so that it's at a very gentle simmer. Simmer gently for 40 minutes, or until you have a thick ketchup consistency.

Remove from the heat and discard the bay leaves. Blitz the mixture with a stick blender until you have a smooth consistency. Set aside and allow to cool completely.

When the mixture is ready, add 1 tablespoon of your ferment starter to it, then using a funnel, transfer the mixture to your glass jar. Gently pour the second tablespoon of ferment on top of the ketchup, so that it seals the ketchup from the air. Fix a round piece of waxed paper over the top of the mouth of the jar, and secure with a rubber band. This will stop critters from flying or crawling into the sauce while it ferments.

Sit the ferment somewhere on your worktop, and allow it to ferment for up to five days.

Remove the paper and replace with the lid to the jar and refrigerate. The sauce will continue to ferment, but the rate will be slowed by the cooler temperatures in the fridge. It will last for several months, and become more sour as the weeks go by. If it gets too sour for your liking, add another spoonful of maple syrup to balance it out.

Oli's favorite teriyaki sauce.

SERVES 2-3

Teriyaki sauce is another one that is really easy to make yourself, and it's a firm favorite with the children, as my son Oli will testify. The Japanese use teriyaki to glaze or baste dishes, which gives a distinctive sheen as well as flavor. It's wonderful with a piece of grilled salmon or chicken, or you can pour it over pan-fried tempeh (healthier than tofu). Serve alongside some cooked quinoa (see page 159) and some steamed greens (page 48).

The important thing here is to source really good-quality tamari and mirin. Most of the commercially available soy sauces and mirin in the supermarkets are full of GM soy products, high-fructose corn syrup, flavorings, and preservatives. Traditionally brewed varieties have amazing flavor and health benefits without all the nasty stuff.

4-5 tablespoons tamari or shoyu (traditionally brewed Japanese dark soy sauce)
4-5 tablespoons mirin (a form of rice wine—Clearspring does a great version)
Zest and juice of 1 lime
2 tablespoons maple syrup
1 fat garlic clove, finely sliced
A chunk of ginger, peeled and finely sliced

Put everything in a small saucepan and bring to a boil. Turn down the heat and simmer until the sauce reduces and has become a bit sticky. Scoop out the garlic and ginger pieces. Taste for seasoning, adjusting if necessary—it may need a little more lime or maple syrup. Pour over a juicy, perfectly cooked steak, or a piece of broiled or pan-fried salmon, veggies, or tempeh. Serve with your favorite greens and some quinoa.

Sweet chili sauce.

MAKES 1 PINT JAR

Most store-bought sweet chili sauce is full of sugar, whereas this recipe, using honey, is healthier, while still giving you all the flavor and kick of the bottled version. Unsurprisingly, it is great with rice, noodles, spring rolls, rice paper rolls, tempura, and other wonderful Asian-inspired dishes, but it also goes well with some cheeses and roast winter veggies.

EQUIPMENT
Sterilized glass jar with an airtight lid (see page 79)

10 long red chiles
4 garlic cloves, crushed
3 tablespoons fresh ginger, peeled and finely grated
¾ cup apple cider vinegar
Scant 1 cup light clear honey
A good pinch of sea salt

Halve the chiles lengthwise, remove the seeds, and discard (you can add them if you wish, but the sauce will be even hotter). Thinly slice the chiles on the diagonal, or finely chop them.

Put all the ingredients in a medium saucepan over low heat. Simmer gently, stirring until well combined. Then allow to simmer for an additional 10–15 minutes, or until the sauce has thickened and is slightly syrupy.

Transfer to the jar and allow to cool before popping it into the fridge. The sauce will keep for well over a month.

Pesto a few ways.

SERVES 4-6

I love homemade pesto as a dip, as a dressing, in sandwiches, on roast veggies, on hearty stews, tossed through zucchini ribbons, or on rye toast with soft cheese and arugula. The pine nuts and olive oil are "good fats" that nourish the brain; the garlic and herbs aid digestion and are sources of micronutrients—vitamins and minerals that are essential for our bodies to produce enzymes and hormones that promote growth and development. So get creative, and add it to your savory dishes to bring them to life.

CLASSIC PESTO
1 garlic clove, chopped
3 handfuls of freshly
    washed basil leaves,
    picked and chopped
A handful of pine nuts,
    lightly toasted
¾ cup finely grated
    Parmesan cheese (or a
    mature Pecorino)
⅔ cup extra virgin olive oil
A squeeze of lemon
Sea salt and freshly
    ground black pepper

Put the garlic, basil, pine nuts, Parmesan, and olive oil into a blender and blitz into a rough sauce. Add a squeeze of lemon, then season to taste. This will keep, covered, in the fridge for up to one week.

**KALE AND CASHEW
PESTO**
¾ cup cashew nuts, lightly
    toasted
¾ cup grated Parmesan
    cheese
2 garlic cloves
⅓ cup extra virgin olive oil
3 ounces kale, green leafy
    parts only, not the inner
    stalk
A squeeze of lemon
Sea salt and freshly
    ground black pepper

Put everything into a blender and blitz into a rough sauce. Season and add more lemon juice or Parmesan if needed.

WALNUT PESTO
1¾ cups walnut pieces
1 garlic clove
1 cup finely grated
    Parmesan cheese
A handful of parsley, basil,
    or kale
⅔ cup extra virgin olive oil
Sea salt and freshly
    ground black pepper

Place everything into a blender and blitz into a rough sauce. Adjust the balance with a little extra cheese or oil. Season.

My favorite salsa verde.

SERVES 4-6

Salsa verde literally means 'green sauce'. I LOVE this stuff—you can adapt it to whatever you are eating, be it veggies, chicken, fish, or broiled meat, by adjusting the herbs accordingly. I use tarragon or dill in place of mint if I want to make this sauce to go with fish; rosemary instead of basil would be a natural pairing with lamb. Because salsa verde uses fresh herbs, use it the day you make it for the best color and flavor.

---

2 garlic cloves
A small handful of capers
    (not the salted ones)
7 anchovy fillets
3 handfuls of flat-leaf
    parsley, leaves picked
A bunch of fresh basil,
    leaves picked
A handful of fresh mint,
    leaves picked
1 tablespoon Dijon
    mustard
3 tablespoons red wine
    vinegar
⅔ cup really good extra
    virgin olive oil
Sea salt and freshly
    ground black pepper

The traditional and best way to make salsa verde is to chop the garlic, capers, anchovies, and herbs really finely by hand. Put them into a bowl and add the mustard and vinegar, then slowly stir in the olive oil until you get the desired consistency. Taste and adjust the flavors with salt and pepper—you may need a bit more vinegar.

Alternatively, you can make this sauce by simply putting everything into a blender, and blitzing to a lovely green sauce, but be careful not to make it too smooth. Taste and adjust the seasoning as necessary.

Serve fresh. I find it tastes best eaten within a day or two.

Fig and date chutney.

MAKES ABOUT 2 PINTS

Deeply delicious, rich brown, sour-sweet fig chutney to tickle the tastebuds and delight the palate. This is one of my absolute favorite chutneys and it is always the one my son and I reach for when we want to enjoy a fine piece of cheese. Make it in late summer, when fresh figs are plentiful—especially if you're lucky enough to have your own tree. Fresh figs can be expensive in the supermarkets, so try to find them at the farmers' market or fruit and vedge store where they tend to be cheaper. This recipe really is at its best when the figs are bursting with ripeness.

EQUIPMENT

Several sterilized glass jars with lids (see page 79)

2¼ pounds fresh figs
1¼ cups cider vinegar
heaping 2 cups onions, chopped
scant 2 cups golden raisins
5 Medjool dates, pitted and chopped

1 teaspoon sea salt
½ teaspoon ground cinnamon
½ teaspoon ground cloves
½ teaspoon cracked black peppercorns
1 teaspoon coriander seeds
Scant 2 cups coconut sugar or unrefined cane sugar

Stem and coarsely chop the figs, place them in a large stainless steel or enameled saucepan. Add the rest of the ingredients except the sugar, and bring the mix to a boil. Simmer for 30–35 minutes until the onions and fruit are soft.

Add the coconut sugar. Bring the fragrant mixture slowly back to a boil, then turn the heat down and simmer very, very gently so that the pan only just bubbles. Cook for an additional 15 minutes, giving the chutney the occasional stir to prevent it sticking to the bottom. When the mixture is thick and jam-like, remove it from the heat, ladle into the jars. While hot, put the lids on and process in a boiling-water bath according to the jar manufacturer's instructions. If sealed well, this chutney can last for months on the pantry shelf.

Serve with delicious cheeses, homemade breads, and other yummy savory things.

My classic apple and pear chutney with ginger.

MAKES ABOUT 2 PINTS

This chutney is great to make when you have apples falling off the tree and you can't eat any more crumble. It makes a great gift, and even though it appears to have a lot of sugar, you only eat a small amount at a time. Plus, if you use unrefined cane sugar, it contains molasses, and that makes the chutney more nutritious. Bramley apples work best here, but you can also use Granny Smith apples in the absence of a good, tart cooking apple.

EQUIPMENT

Clean piece of cheesecloth
Several sterilized glass jars with lids (see page 79)

1½ pounds cooking apples, peeled, cored, and roughly chopped
10 ounces pears, peeled, cored and roughly chopped
3–4 medium red onions, finely chopped
5 garlic cloves, peeled and finely chopped
¾ cup golden raisins, roughly chopped
12 dates, pitted and chopped

¾ cup ginger, grated
3 large pieces candied ginger, thinly sliced
2 teaspoons sea salt
3¼ cups apple cider vinegar
3¾ cups unrefined cane sugar (or coconut sugar, or honey)

PICKLING SPICES
5 teaspoons coriander seeds
1 teaspoon yellow mustard seeds
1 teaspoon fennel seeds
8 whole cloves
2 teaspoons black peppercorns
2 teaspoons cumin seeds

Put the pickling spices on a clean piece of cheesecloth. Bring up the sides, and tie with thin string. Add it to a large, heavy-bottomed preserving pan along with all the prepared ingredients and salt, and pour over the apple cider vinegar.

Bring the pan slowly to a boil, then reduce the heat and simmer gently for 30–45 minutes, stirring once in a while, until pulpy and soft. Add the sugar, and allow it to dissolve in the hot liquid. Continue to cook gently for about 1½–2 hours, stirring every so often, so the chutney does not stick to the pan.

Turn off the heat, and fish out the cheesecloth bag. Transfer the chutney into hot sterilized jars. Put the lids on and process in a boiling-water bath according to the jar manufacturer's instructions. Store in the pantry for 2–3 months before opening, then keep refrigerated and consume within 1 year.

Charred cherry tomato and chili salsa.

SERVES 6-8

This is my favorite, super-easy, classic Mexican salsa made with chargrilled cherry tomatoes. It's delicious with broiled fish, slow-cooked pork tacos, avocado on toast, or with crispy roast chicken (see page 53) with a side of guacamole and a green salad.

1½ pounds cherry tomatoes, washed and dried	2 tablespoons freshly squeezed lime juice
3–4 whole fresh serrano or jalapeño chiles, stemmed	A handful of chopped cilantro
3 medium garlic cloves, peeled	½ red onion, finely diced
1 teaspoon sea salt	Generous drizzle of extra virgin olive oil
	Sea salt and freshly ground black pepper

Put the tomatoes on a large foil-lined baking sheet and place under a preheated broiler for 10–15 minutes until they are softened and blackened in spots. Set aside to cool a little.

Set a large skillet over low–medium heat. Roast the chiles in the dry pan, turning occasionally, until they are blistered all over and blackened in spots. Remove and set aside to cool a little.

Slip the skins from the tomatoes, and using a small sharp paring knife, gently scrape the skins from the chiles. (You don't need to be too meticulous—some burnt bits add extra flavor, which I love.)

Use a mortar and pestle to pound the garlic with the roasted chiles and salt to a paste. Transfer to a bowl, add the tomatoes, and give a gentle stir to coat, mashing very lightly with a fork to break up the tomatoes a little. Add the lime juice, cilantro, and onion, and drizzle over the oil. Stir once more and season to taste.

You can make this salsa up to 12 hours before you want to use it.

Oma's tomato kasundi relish.

MAKES ABOUT 3¼ QUARTS

I first tasted kasundi relish when I worked in an amazing bakery in Melbourne called Babka. It has a lovely warmth and beautiful depth of flavor. Try it with barbecued meats, fried eggs, or cheese on toast. This particular recipe comes from a dear friend, Marguerite Guinness, a wizard in the kitchen, and in the garden too. Marguerite always makes her kasundi relish in late summer, when her garden is overflowing with sweet, sun-ripened tomatoes. If you want to make it thicker, and more intensely flavored, cook it for a little longer than the recommended time, so that it reduces even further; either way it's delicious and addictive.

EQUIPMENT	
Several sterilized glass jars with lids (see page 79)	2 tablespoons ground coriander
	1½ cups minced fresh ginger
Scant ¼ cup cumin seeds, lightly toasted	2 bulbs garlic peeled and crushed
⅞ cup ghee or cold-pressed sunflower oil	5½ pounds large fresh tomatoes, chopped
⅓ cup mustard seeds	3 cups coconut sugar
2 tablespoons ground turmeric	2 cups + 2 tablespoons malt vinegar
4 tablespoons chili powder	3 tablespoons sea salt
	Freshly ground black pepper

Lightly crush the cumin seeds using a mortar and pestle. Set aside.

Put the ghee or oil in a large saucepan over medium–high heat. Add the mustard and cumin seeds, and cook until they start to pop and sizzle. Reduce the heat, and add the other spices. Cook for an additional minute until the spices release their fragrant aromas.

Add the remaining ingredients, stir to combine, and simmer gently for 1½ hours, or until the relish has thickened. Transfer to the jars and screw the lids on while still hot. This relish will last for months, if not all winter. Once opened, keep refrigerated.

Pico de gallo.

SERVES 4–6

I am totally in love with this stuff; it's great with a Mexican feast, but so, so good with many other things too. Pico de gallo is simply a Mexican fresh tomato salsa. Tomatoes are packed with lycopene, a phytochemical that helps protect against cancer, and the raw onions and garlic are full of prebiotics—a particular kind of fiber that probiotics, the healthy yeast and bacteria, feed on—so with each tasty mouthful, you are providing the microflora in your gut with all the good stuff it needs. I love serving this as a side salad with avocado and eggs on rye toast. It's a cinch to make, and the results far surpass the effort needed to throw it together.

10 ounces heritage and cherry tomatoes
1 medium red chile, finely diced
1 medium green chile, finely diced
1 small red onion, finely diced
1 garlic clove, finely grated

Juice of 1 lime
Zest and juice of ½ lemon
A small bunch of cilantro, roughly chopped
A small dash of olive oil
Sea salt and freshly ground black pepper

Chop the heritage tomatoes into small pieces, and cut the cherry tomatoes into either halves or quarters, depending on size. Put them into a large bowl along with all the other ingredients, season, and mix thoroughly.

Transfer to a serving bowl, and keep refrigerated until ready to use. It's best eaten soon after it's made.

Beet and ginger chutney.

MAKES ABOUT 2¾ POUNDS

This is a favorite chutney of mine. It is wonderfully fragrant, and will fill your kitchen with its aroma as you cook it. I love beets, and making chutney is a great way to use up a glut. I sometimes give this chutney for Christmas presents; it goes so beautifully with cold meats and festive leftovers.

EQUIPMENT
Several sterilized glass jars with lids (see page 79)

18 ounces fresh beets, peeled and chopped into small cubes
2¼ pounds cooking apples, peeled, quartered, cored and roughly chopped
2 large red onions, roughly chopped

2 teaspoons freshly grated ginger
5 large pieces candied ginger, finely chopped
2⅔ cups unrefined cane or coconut sugar
2 teaspoons sea salt
½ teaspoon ground cinnamon
½ teaspoon ground cloves
1 teaspoon ground cumin
3¼ cups red wine vinegar

Put the beets, apples, and red onions into a large pan. Add the fresh ginger, stem ginger, sugar, salt, and spices. Pour in the vinegar, and stir well to mix. Bring to a boil, then turn the heat down and simmer for about 1 hour. Stir every now and then to prevent the chutney from sticking to the bottom of the pan.

After 1 hour the chutney should be ready, and the beets lovely and tender. Spoon into the jars. While hot, screw the lids on.

If sealed well, the chutney should last several months, if not all winter. Once opened, keep refrigerated and consume within three weeks. Serve with cheeses, cold meats, salad sandwiches, homemade quiches, or vegetable tarts.

Hummus a few ways.

SERVES 4-6

Hummus is a great thing: kids love it, adults love it—I don't know anyone who doesn't love it. There are some quite decent store-bought ones, but I much prefer the taste of my own hummus, and I also know that it has the best-quality oils in it, not bad fats, which are one of the worst things anyone, children especially, can eat for many reasons. Bad fats, such as processed oils, which are found in pretty much all store-bought dips, contain trans fats, which are highly toxic, and should be avoided at all costs. With a homemade hummus, you get the best of everything, and it's more delicious. Win win. The basic recipe uses chickpeas, but you can vary that by adding roasted vegetable purées very successfully, as I show here.

BASIC HUMMUS RECIPE

7 ounces jarred/canned chickpeas, drained
2 tablespoons lemon juice, or more to taste
2 garlic cloves, finely grated
1 teaspoon ground cumin
Generous ⅓ cup tahini
2 tablespoons extra virgin olive oil, plus a little extra to serve
Sea salt

TO GARNISH
1 teaspoon paprika
1 tablespoon finely chopped curly-leaf parsley

Put everything into a food processor along with 4 tablespoons of cold water and blitz until smooth (or use a bowl and stick blender, and save yourself the task of washing the food processor). Season to taste.

Spoon into a bowl and use the back of the spoon to smooth the surface and create a lovely swirl on the top. Sprinkle with the paprika and parsley, then drizzle a little extra oil on top.

Roasted red pepper hummus with chipotle.
Follow the basic recipe, but omit the cumin and water, and add 2 roasted red bell peppers, skinned and seeded, and 1½ teaspoons of chipotle powder. Blitz until you have a lovely smooth hummus.

Season to taste, and finish as usual, but replace the paprika and parsley garnish with a sprinkle of extra chipotle powder.

Roasted pumpkin and sumac hummus.
Follow the basic recipe, but omit the water, and add 3½ ounces roasted butternut squash. Blitz until you have a lovely smooth hummus.

Season to taste. Finish as usual, but sprinkle with ½ teaspoon of sumac instead of paprika.

Roasted carrot and turmeric hummus.
Follow the basic recipe, but omit the water, and add a handful of roasted carrot pieces and 1 teaspoon of ground turmeric. Blitz until smooth, and garnish with plenty of good extra virgin olive oil and chopped curly-leaf parsley.

Cashew and artichoke dip.

SERVES 8-10

This is a delicious dip and one I have made for many parties. Artichokes are one of the most nutrient-dense vedge you can eat, and they also contain lots of prebiotics. Raw cashew nuts are a great source of minerals, fiber, protein, and unsaturated fat, making this dip a winning combination.

1 cup raw cashew nuts, soaked in room-temperature water for at least 1 hour and up to 4 hours
14 ounces roasted artichoke hearts (you can make your own, or use jarred roasted artichoke hearts in oil)
Juice of 1 lemon
½ red onion, finely diced
½–1 teaspoon cayenne pepper
¼ teaspoon paprika
½ teaspoon ground sumac
3 smallish garlic cloves, minced
A small bunch of flat-leaf parsley, stalks removed and leaves finely chopped, plus extra to garnish
A few good glugs of extra virgin olive oil
Sea salt and freshly ground black pepper

Drain and rinse the cashew nuts several times under cold running water.

Blend all the ingredients in a high-powered blender or food processor until completely smooth, thick, and creamy, adding a glug of olive oil at a time to get just the right consistency. You are looking for a smooth, creamy dip that holds its shape quite well.

Scrape the mix into a beautiful serving bowl, and sprinkle with parsley, and perhaps an extra dusting of sumac, and a final drizzle of olive oil.

Keep refrigerated until ready to serve. This dip will last a few days in the fridge if covered.

White bean purée with roasted garlic, rosemary, and sumac.

SERVES 10 AS A DIP

This delicious white bean purée is a wonderful way to use beans. It's incredible served instead of mashed potato, and it's amazing as a dip, or part of a mezze platter. You can also make little crostini, and serve this on top as a canapé, perhaps with some crispy prosciutto, and a fried sage leaf. Divine.

2 large whole bulbs of garlic
3–4 good-sized rosemary sprigs
1–2 tablespoons ghee
28 ounces canned navy beans, drained and rinsed
3 tablespoons extra virgin olive oil, plus extra to serve
Juice of ½ lemon
1 teaspoon ground sumac, to serve
Sea salt and freshly ground black pepper

Preheat the oven to 325°F.

Start by roasting the garlic: put the whole bulbs in a small dish with the rosemary, and drizzle with 1 tablespoon of the ghee. Wrap the dish in foil. Bake for about 1 hour, or until the garlic is very tender.

Remove the garlic from the oven. Cool a little, and then squeeze the soft garlic paste from the cloves into a food processor, discarding the skins. Remove the roasted rosemary leaves from their stalks and pop the leaves into the food processor too, discarding the stalks, and drizzle in any garlic oil from the roasting dish.

Next add the beans, olive oil, and lemon juice to the food processor. Blend to a coarse purée. Add a little more oil or warm water to thin the mix if it is too stiff. Taste, season with salt and black pepper, and add more lemon juice as necessary. Scoop into a beautiful dish, and sprinkle with the sumac and an extra drizzle of olive oil and ghee to serve.

Burnt eggplant with pomegranate molasses.

SERVES 6-8

This is my take on the Lebanese classic *baba ganoush*: it's smoky and decadent, and insanely good with that creamy quality that a good eggplant dip should have. It is the perfect accompaniment to roast meats, or hearty autumnal vedge.

1 large or 2 smaller eggplants	½ teaspoon ground cumin
⅔ cup Greek yogurt, at room temperature	A pinch of cayenne pepper
2 tablespoons extra virgin olive oil	1 garlic clove, finely minced or crushed
1½ teaspoons pomegranate molasses	Seeds of ½ pomegranate
2 tablespoons lemon juice	2 tablespoons finely chopped curly-leaf parsley, to garnish
1 teaspoon ground sumac	Sea salt and freshly ground black pepper

Start by placing the eggplant over a moderate flame. This works amazingly well and takes a fraction of the time broiling would—although it requires thorough cleaning of the stovetop afterward. Once the eggplant is on the flame, burn it for 12–14 minutes, turning every now and then, using metal tongs so that it cooks on all sides. (To broil it instead, put the eggplant under a hot broiler for 40–60 minutes, depending on the size. Turn occasionally, and keep an eye on it—you don't want the skin to burn to a crisp before the inside is cooked, which takes a surprisingly long time under the broiler). It is done when the skin dries and cracks, and smoky aromas are released. As it cooks, you will see the eggplant collapsing within its skin. When the eggplant is done, remove it from the heat and set aside to cool a little.

Make a long cut down the length of the eggplant and open it up. Use a spoon to scoop out the cooked flesh, avoiding most of the burnt skin, although a little is nice for a smoky flavor. Put the flesh in a strainer or colander for 10 minutes, to allow some of the liquid to drain, then transfer to a board and chop roughly. It's important to let it dry out a bit in the strainer, or the dip will be soggy.

Transfer the eggplant to a mixing bowl, and add the remaining ingredients, but reserve half the pomegranate seeds. Give everything a good stir to thoroughly combine, and then taste and season. Scoop into a serving bowl, and sprinkle with the parsley and reserved pomegranate seeds.

Black olive tapenade.

MAKES 1 SMALL BOWL

Tapenade is a wonderful little dish—dark and sophisticated, deeply delicious, and perfect served with some crudités and a stiff drink at sunset on a warm summery evening. You can make tapenade with green olives and other things like sun-dried tomatoes, but I prefer the more traditional way of just using black olives. Try to buy the olives that still have their pits in; you won't regret it because they are far superior in taste and only take a moment to pit.

12 ounces whole black Kalamata olives, pitted	2½ tablespoons fresh thyme, leaves only, chopped
4 anchovies, well rinsed if packed in salt, roughly chopped	Juice of ½ lemon, plus a little extra if needed
2 medium cloves garlic, crushed	7–8 tablespoons extra virgin olive oil
3½ tablespoons capers, rinsed	Freshly ground black pepper
1 tablespoon chopped curly-leaf parsley	

Put the olives in a food processor with the anchovies, garlic, capers, parsley, and thyme. Whizz to a rough purée, being careful not to let the mixture get too fine—some texture is a good thing here. Add the lemon juice, and with the motor still running, slowly trickle in the oil—enough to get the desired consistency. Stop the motor, remove the lid, grind a few really good twists of black pepper, and taste, adding more lemon juice or pepper as needed.

Scrape into a bowl and enjoy immediately, or refrigerate until ready to use. This delicious dip will last a good few days if kept cool.

Serve as part of an antipasti platter, or with crackers and/or crudités for dipping. This makes a relatively small amount, but a little goes a long way.

My roasted red pepper and rosemary spread.

SERVES 4 AS A SIDE, MORE AS A DIP

I first came across the idea for this spread in David Frenkiel and Luise Vindahl's *Green Kitchen* cookbook. It is so delicious I wanted to make my own version, and I now keep a jar of this in my fridge at all times. It's perfect on rye toast with avocado and salad, or as a dip with seasonal crudités. I also serve it with roast vedge or a broiled piece of fish. The seeds add lots of good oils, and pumpkin seeds in particular contain lots of zinc—great for balancing the hormones and clearing the skin.

3 red bell peppers, halved
   and seeded
Olive oil
Generous ⅓ cup sunflower
   seeds
Generous ⅓ cup pumpkin
   seeds

A pinch of smoked
   paprika
Juice of ½ lemon
2 rosemary sprigs,
   leaves only
A hearty pinch of sea
   salt and freshly ground
   black pepper

Preheat the oven to 400°F. Put the red bell peppers on a roasting pan, and drizzle with olive oil. Roast for about 40 minutes, or until slightly charred at the edges, and the skin is easy to peel off. Remove from the oven, and set aside to cool.

Next, lightly toast the seeds in a dry skillet, until they release their delicious nutty aroma and are starting to pop. Transfer them to a bowl.

When the peppers are cool enough to handle, peel off the skins. Put the peppers in a bowl with the remaining ingredients, and blitz with a stick blender until smooth. Taste, and adjust the seasoning if necessary. Scrape the mixture into a glass jar, and keep in the fridge for up to two weeks, if it lasts that long! Mine never does.

A creamy, zesty guacamole.

SERVES 10

This is my favorite guacamole recipe. It's a great way of using up a bunch of avocados for a light lunch. Serve it with a tomato salad, or on sourdough rye toast drizzled with olive oil and rubbed with a clove of garlic—totally yummy!! This recipe makes quite a large amount, so just halve or quarter if you have fewer people to feed.

---

6 ripe avocados, halved and pitted
Zest and juice of 1 lemon
Zest of 1 lime and juice of 2 limes
1 red onion, finely diced
2 garlic cloves, finely grated
2 medium green chiles, seeded and finely chopped
½ cup cold-pressed olive oil (extra virgin is wonderful) plus extra to serve
A small bunch of cilantro, roughly chopped, plus extra sprigs to garnish
Sea salt and freshly ground black pepper

Scoop the flesh of the avocados into a medium bowl, mash with a fork, then squeeze over the lemon and lime juice. Mix, then add all the remaining ingredients. Check the seasoning, adding a little salt and pepper to taste. Scrape into a lovely serving bowl, drizzle with a little olive oil, and garnish with a few sprigs of cilantro.

Smashed peas and fava beans with mint and parsley.

SERVES 4

This little dish of spring delight is fresh and delicate, yet it packs a serious flavor punch. Great as a dip, but also amazing on sourdough toast with a poached egg and a sprinkle of arugula leaves, or pea shoots. Make it during the short season when fresh fava beans are available—they're full of vitamin C.

A small handful of mint leaves
A few parsley sprigs, leaves only
4–5 basil leaves
A large handful of fresh or frozen peas (lightly thawed if using frozen)
A handful of fresh or frozen fava beans (lightly thawed if using frozen), podded and skinned
1 fat garlic clove, peeled
A large handful of finely grated Pecorino (or Parmesan cheese)
Extra virgin olive oil
Juice of ½ lemon
A tangle of fresh pea shoots, to serve
Sea salt and freshly ground black pepper

Use a mortar and pestle or a food processor to smash the mint, parsley, and basil with the peas, beans, and garlic until it all looks lovely and mushy.

Add the Pecorino, then loosen the whole mix with a few good glugs of good-quality olive oil, and balance out the flavors with a little lemon juice, salt, and pepper before serving.

Chicken liver pâté.

MAKES 2 BOWLS / SERVES 15

2¾ sticks unsalted butter
Ghee or an extra knob of
  butter
3 shallots or ½ red onion,
  minced
3 fat garlic cloves, minced
1 pound high-welfare
  chicken livers, trimmed
  (free-range and not
  corn-fed)

A few sprigs of fresh sage,
  leaves picked
½ teaspoon thyme leaves,
  finely chopped
½ cup Marsala wine
½ teaspoon ground ginger
Sea salt and freshly
  ground black pepper

Place half the butter in a small saucepan over medium–low heat for about 10 minutes until separated, with milk solids at the top and bottom and clarified butter in the middle. Strain off the solids, and pour the clarified butter into a clean bowl.

Heat a little ghee, or a knob of butter in a large skillet. Gently fry the shallots and garlic for 10 minutes until soft. Transfer to a plate. Wipe the pan clean, increase the heat, then add the livers, and most of the sage and the thyme leaves in a single layer. Cook the livers for 2 minutes on each side, until lightly colored, but still pink in the middle. If they are fully cooked, they can make the pâté grainy. Carefully scoop the livers and herbs from the pan and set aside.

Keeping the pan on the heat, carefully pour in the Marsala. Simmer for about 1 minute to reduce, then take off the heat and pour into a food processor along with the shallots, garlic, ginger, and livers. Blitz to a smooth purée. Add the remaining butter, and continue to blitz, pulsing if necessary, then season to taste.

Transfer the mixture into two serving bowls. Lay the remaining sage leaves over the pâté, then carefully pour over the clarified butter. Leave to set in the fridge for at least 2 hours—it tastes even better after a couple of days. If left undisturbed, the pâté will keep for a good 10 days.

Liver is one of nature's most potent superfoods. It's so nutrient-dense that it contains a larger amount of micronutrients than almost all fruit and veggies, and even red meat. When cooking and eating livers it is very important to use livers that come from pasture-raised animals.

The reason for this is that you want good, clean healthy livers that haven't become a dumping ground for all the chemicals and GM feed and hormones that you get with factory-farmed chickens. Free-range and organic livers are best: dark in color and fresh as you can find them. This meltingly soft pâté goes beautifully with my spiced almond crackers (see page 157).

Deeply delicious walnut and lentil pâté.

SERVES 6-8

Perfect for topping little crostini or my crackers on page 157 for easy party canapés. Walnuts are full of essential fatty acids and healthy fats, and they make a delicious pâté.

---

2 tablespoons ghee
1 medium red onion, chopped
1 celery stalk (use a middle one), finely chopped
2 bay leaves
3½ ounces walnuts (about 1 cup), soaked for a minimum of 4 hours, then drained and rinsed
1 tablespoon fresh thyme and oregano leaves, mixed, finely chopped
1 cup Puy lentils, cooked

2 tablespoons tamari or shoyu (traditionally fermented soy sauce)
2 tablespoons lemon juice
3 tablespoons extra virgin olive oil, plus extra for drizzling
1-2 teaspoons traditionally brewed white miso paste (optional)
½ teaspoon smoked paprika, plus extra for sprinkling
Sea salt and freshly ground black pepper

Preheat the oven to 325°F. Put a medium skillet over moderate heat and warm the ghee. Add the onion, celery, and bay leaves, turn the heat down to low, and cook for 12–15 minutes until the veggies are softened and caramelized. Stir every few minutes so the onions don't catch and burn.

Meanwhile, toast the walnuts. Scatter the nuts on a baking sheet, and pop them into the oven for 10–15 minutes, or until crispy and turning golden. Keep an eye on them as they can burn very easily, and depending on your oven, may take less time. Stir halfway through the roasting, so that they toast evenly on all sides. When they are done, remove them from the oven, and set aside to cool.

Remove the bay leaves, and season the onion mixture with salt and pepper (if you are using miso you won't need much salt). Tip into a high-powered blender, along with the lentils, walnuts, tamari, lemon juice, olive oil, and miso, if using. Blitz to a smooth, creamy consistency. Add the paprika to taste, and mix again. Scrape into a serving bowl, sprinkle with a little extra paprika, and finish with a final drizzle of olive oil and a few good twists of the pepper mill.

Smoked mackerel pâté.

SERVES 6-8

Mackerel pâté is truly delicious: creamy yet tangy, and delightfully addictive. It's great on toasted rye pumpernickel bread, or even cucumber rounds, or scooped into little gem lettuce cups. Mackerel is an oily fish which is full of vitamin D, some B vitamins, selenium, and it also contains omega-3 essential fatty acids, all of which means eating this humble fish is great for brain health. I am sure other smoked fish would work just as well in this recipe, too. For instance, last summer I was staying with friends in New Zealand, and the kids caught an eel, which we first smoked, and then used to make this pâté in place of the mackerel fillets.

---

3 medium or 4 smaller hot-smoked mackerel fillets
1 cup crème fraîche (you can use sour cream but you may need extra lemon juice)
1 tablespoon freshly grated horseradish (if you can't find any, omit and add ½–1 teaspoon Dijon mustard)

Juice of 1 lemon
A small handful of dill, stalks removed, finely chopped
A small handful of parsley, leaves picked and very finely chopped
Sea salt and freshly ground black pepper

Turn the mackerel fillets skin-side up, carefully peel off the skin and do a quick check for bones, carefully removing any—the bones can be quite small, so check thoroughly!

Flake most of the fish into a food processor, reserving about one-third or a bit less. Add the crème fraîche and horseradish or mustard, and blitz until smooth. You can also just mash these three ingredients in a bowl using a fork (less cleaning up!).

Add salt, a good grinding of black pepper, and the lemon juice, then fold through the dill, parsley, and remaining fish, leaving some in lovely big flakes to give a pleasing texture.

Keep the pâté refrigerated until you're ready to serve. It will last well in the fridge for a few days if covered.

Tip: If you have any chive flowers on hand, they look beautiful sprinkled on top. They are a lovely light purple color and lend beauty and a fiery flavor to this dish.

Gremolata—2 ways.

MAKES ENOUGH TO SPRINKLE OVER 2 DISHES

Gremolata with parsley.

I love this stuff—it elevates something from plain to totally amazing, with one small sprinkle. Genius.

I add it to soups, salads, open sandwiches, and roasted veggies, particularly carrots, parsnips, pumpkins, and sweet potatoes. It's great on meat before or after roasting, fish, chicken... pretty much everything. I love it every which way. Making gremolata is also a great way of using up parsley that would otherwise get left in the vedge drawer of your fridge, and inevitably go yellow and be thrown away. This way you get something totally delicious and nothing gets wasted.

A bunch of flat-leaf parsley, washed, leaves picked and finely chopped	1 big fat garlic clove or 2 small ones, peeled and minced
	Zest of 2 unwaxed lemons

Make sure you thoroughly dry the parsley after washing, because if the leaves are wet, the gremolata will have a soggy ending.

Simply toss all the ingredients in a bowl. That's it, so simple. Gremolata keeps well in the fridge for a couple of days, but ensure it's covered with plastic wrap, or in an airtight jar.

Gremolata with mustard greens.

My mom grows the most delicious mustard greens. I used to wander through her garden and pick all the baby salad leaves, and mustard greens were one of my favorites, so mustardy and peppery. Delicious. Use them in place of the parsley in this recipe for a different flavor note.

Pistachio and kale ash dukkah.

MAKES 1–2 HALF-PINT JARS

Dukkah is a delicious spice blend, amazing sprinkled onto an omelet or scrambled eggs, or avocado on toast. It's also great served in a small bowl alongside another bowl of really good quality-olive oil and a pile of fresh hot pita breads. You dip a piece of pita first into the oil, then into the dukkah. Make sure your seeds and spices are really fresh for the full flavor hit.

A large handful of curly kale, thick stems removed	4 tablespoons cumin seeds
¾ cup pistachios	2 teaspoons fennel seeds
7 tablespoons coriander seeds	2 tablespoons black peppercorns
6 tablespoons sesame seeds	2 teaspoons dried mint leaves
	2 teaspoons sea salt flakes

Preheat the oven to 350°F. Put the kale leaves onto a baking sheet big enough to hold them in a single layer and bake them for about 5 minutes, then reduce the heat to 225°F and dry them out for an additional 5 minutes, or until the kale crumbles easily, but retains its bright green color. Remove from the oven, and let cool completely before scrunching it up in your hands to create a fine powder. Store in a jar with a tight-fitting lid. You won't need all of it.

Heat a heavy-bottomed pan over high heat, add the pistachios and dry-fry until slightly browned and fragrant. Watch them carefully, as they can burn easily. Remove from the heat, and cool completely. Repeat with each of the seeds and peppercorns. To speed things up, you can do all the seeds together, but do the sesame seeds separately as they take much less time. Allow them to cool completely.

Grind or blitz the nuts, seeds, mint, and salt in a mortar or mini blender until the mix is of a coarse consistency. DO NOT allow it to become a paste. You want a lovely crumbly spice mix. Transfer to a jar, add 1–2 tablespoons of the kale ash, and give everything a good mix. Stored in an airtight jar, it will keep for up to one month.

For a more traditional dukkah, omit the pistachios and kale ash and replace with hazelnuts.

Moroccan spice mix.

MAKES 1 JAR

This blend of spices is amazing tossed through warm cauliflower couscous, salad, or sprinkled over baby carrots before roasting.

4 tablespoons ground cumin

2 tablespoons each ground coriander, sweet paprika, and dried red pepper flakes

1 teaspoon each dried garlic powder and ground cinnamon

½ teaspoon ground cloves

½ teaspoon freshly ground black pepper

Combine all the ingredients in a small bowl, then transfer to an airtight jar. It will keep for up to 3 months.

Jerk seasoning.

MAKES ENOUGH FOR 1 CHICKEN

This delicious, zesty, spicy marinade is fantastic for roasted or barbecued chicken, pork, and fish. It's also great on hearty chunks of slow-roasted winter veggies.

2 teaspoons fresh or dried chopped parsley

A handful of fresh thyme leaves

2 cinnamon sticks, crushed

3 tablespoons chopped fresh cilantro

1 tablespoon coriander seeds

2 tablespoons crushed black peppercorns

1 teaspoon freshly grated nutmeg

1 tablespoon crushed allspice

7 garlic cloves

3 Scotch bonnet chiles, seeded

1 tablespoon chopped ginger

1 teaspoon paprika

Zest of 1 lime and juice of 2 limes

2 teaspoons coconut or palm sugar

1 teaspoon salt

⅔ cup fruity olive oil

Place all the ingredients into a food processor and blitz until you have a smooth paste. Transfer to an airtight container and refrigerate until needed. It will keep, chilled, for up to 2 weeks.

Piri piri spice mix.

MAKES 1 JAR

Add some fire to a paneer steak, a spatchcock chicken, or roast vegetables with this spicy blend.

4 tablespoons smoked paprika

1 tablespoon each dried oregano and red pepper flakes

4 teaspoons turmeric

2 tablespoons dried parsley

2 teaspoons each sea salt and garlic powder

½ teaspoon freshly ground black pepper

Combine all the ingredients in small bowl, then transfer to an airtight jar. It will keep for up to 3 months.

Ras el-hanout.

MAKES 1 JAR

North African in origin, this spice blend has a deep, warm flavor, with a kick of chile, rounded off with floral notes from the rose petals. Sprinkle it over fish, chicken, or roasted veggies.

3 cinnamon sticks, broken into several pieces

2 tablespoons each coriander and cumin seeds

1½ tablespoons fenugreek

1½ tablespoons mustard seeds

1½ tablespoons whole cloves

1½ tablespoons fennel seeds

2 teaspoons black peppercorns

2 ounces dried Damascan rose petals (from Middle-Eastern food stores, or you can find them online)

Put all the ingredients, except the petals, in a dry heavy-bottomed skillet, and place over low–medium heat. Heat until the seeds begin to pop and release their amazing aromas. Toss and cook for 2 more minutes—don't let them burn, but some gentle color is good. Tip into a coffee grinder, spice grinder, mini food processor, or mortar and pestle, and grind while still warm, but not hot. Add the dried rose petals and crush lightly, so that you still have some texture to the petals. It will keep in an airtight container for 1–2 weeks.

Mediterranean dried herb mix.

MAKES 1 SMALL JAR

Sprinkle over chicken, lamb, goat, or rabbit before roasting or broiling, or try it with halloumi or paneer.

1 tablespoon dried parsley	1 teaspoon garlic powder
1 tablespoon dried basil	1 teaspoon sea salt flakes
2 teaspoons dried	or pink Himalayan salt
oregano	1 teaspoon finely grated
2 teaspoons fennel leaves	lemon zest

Combine the parsley, basil, oregano, fennel, and garlic powder in a small bowl. Add the salt, and stir to combine. Just before serving, stir in the lemon zest.

Indian spice mix.

MAKES 1 SMALL JAR

A couple of tablespoons of this handy spice mix makes a base for curries, dahl, warm chickpea salads, roast cauliflower pieces, or roast sweet potato wedges with a bit of ghee. You won't use the entire mix in one go, but make a batch and keep the rest for the next time you want to spice things up.

4 tablespoons cumin	2 teaspoons whole cloves
seeds	4 teaspoons ground
½ teaspoon black	turmeric
peppercorns	1 dried bay leaf
2½ tablespoons coriander	2½ teaspoons ground chili
seeds	powder
4 teaspoons cardamom	1 teaspoon ground
pods	cinnamon

Heat a dry skillet and tip in the cumin, peppercorns, and coriander seeds. Toast for 1–2 minutes, or until their fragrance is released and they are just turning a little golden. Quickly remove from the pan and put into a mortar.

Now toast the cardamom pods for 1–2 minutes, until they are just starting to color, then add them to the mortar along with the cloves and the bay leaf. Use the pestle to grind the seeds and pods into a fine powder. Mix with the rest of the ingredients and then transfer to a jar with a tight-fitting lid.

Za'atar.

MAKES 1 SMALL JAR

This super-easy Middle-Eastern spice blend is beyond versatile. You can sprinkle it over chicken legs or veggies before roasting— try it on sweet potato wedges, carrots, butternut squash, or eggplant. Use it on roasted chickpeas and cauliflower florets to create a satisfying and beautiful warm salad. You can even add it to a jar of vegetables that are being traditionally fermented the wild way. The beauty of this blend is its simplicity. It's so easy to make and gives everything a wonderful flavor.

6 tablespoons fresh thyme	¾ teaspoon sea salt,
leaves	1½ tablespoons toasted
3 teaspoons ground	sesame seeds
sumac	

Preheat the oven to 325°F.

Spread out the thyme leaves on a baking sheet and pop them in the oven to dry for about 10 minutes. When they are done, they should crumble between pinched fingers. Remove the sheet from the oven, and allow to cool.

Grind the thyme leaves finely using a mortar and pestle. Transfer to small bowl.

Add the sumac to the mortar and crush it as finely as you can—you may need to do this in batches. Add the thyme to the sumac and crush them together. Add the salt and crush again.

Stir in the sesame seeds, taste, and adjust the seasoning if desired.

Transfer the spice mix to an airtight jar, and keep in the fridge ready for use. It will last for a couple of weeks.

Rose harissa.

MAKES 2 PINT JARS

This is magic in a jar. The delicate roses balance out the heat of the chiles, and make a warm, fragrant spice paste that is great with oily fish or roasted chicken. It's delicious mixed with my homemade mayo (see pages 72–73) and served with my homemade fries (see page 42), or spread over a shoulder of lamb with fresh fennel (see page 60). Traditionally, this spice paste would have been ground and chopped by hand, but here I use a food processor.

EQUIPMENT
Sterilized jars (see page 79)

12 ounces ripe tomatoes, halved, cores removed
2 red bell peppers, halved and seeded
8 ounces fresh red chiles
8 garlic cloves, unpeeled
2 tablespoons extra virgin olive oil
4 teaspoons cumin seeds
2 teaspoons coriander seeds

1 teaspoon smoked paprika
A handful of unsprayed, fragrant rose petals, washed
8 teaspoons rosewater
2½ tablespoons coconut sugar or unrefined cane sugar, or 3 dried Medjool dates
Juice of 1 lemon
Olive oil
Sea salt and freshly ground black pepper

Preheat the oven to 325°F. Spread in a single layer the tomatoes, cut-side up, red peppers, cut-side down, chiles, and garlic on a large roasting pan, drizzle with the olive oil, and season well. Place the pan in the oven, and roast for 1 hour. Remove from the oven, and set aside to cool.

When the chiles are cool enough to handle, pull off their stalks and seed them. Peel the garlic cloves, and place in the food processor with the chiles. Peel the roasted peppers and pop those in the food processor too. Pulse until roughly chopped, then add the cumin and coriander seeds and paprika, and pulse again.

Next, add the tomatoes, rose petals, rosewater, and sugar or dates, and pulse to create a beautiful, deep-reddish paste. Taste and add more salt and black pepper as needed.

Scrape the paste into a bowl and squeeze in half the lemon juice, add the olive oil, and mix thoroughly. Have a taste— you want a good balance between the heat of the chiles, the smoky paprika, the sharpness of the lemon, and the beautifully fragrant rose petals. Season again if necessary, and add another squeeze of lemon, if needed. Once you're happy with the taste, transfer the mixture into the jars and refrigerate. This paste should keep for 3–4 weeks.

My favorite Thai green curry paste.

SERVES 6-8

This is a fresh, delicious curry paste packed full of flavor. You can add different vedge or meat to turn it into a filling meal. It's super-good for you, as the coconut milk is filling, and full of healthy fats. Coconut milk helps to balance hormones, aids weight loss, feeds the brain, and helps with feelings of satiety. The veggies are full of fiber and micronutrients, the ginger in the paste reduces inflammation in the body, and altogether this humble little dish tastes amazing. I love serving it over cauliflower rice (see page 49).

FOR THE PASTE
5 fat garlic cloves, roughly chopped
3 shallots, roughly chopped
Generous thumb-sized piece of ginger, peeled and roughly chopped
2 lemongrass stalks, tough outer leaves removed, finely chopped
¾-inch piece of galangal (if available), peeled and roughly chopped
5-6 green bird's eye chiles, trimmed
1 teaspoon ground cumin
1 teaspoon ground coriander
¼ teaspoon freshly ground black pepper
½ bunch of fresh cilantro, leaves and stalks
2 tablespoons good-quality fish sauce

FOR THE CURRY
1¾ pounds butternut squash, cut into chunks, or boneless chicken breasts/thighs
Ghee
14 ounces mixed Asian mushrooms, cleaned and torn into even pieces
4 mini eggplants, topped and halved, or 1 large eggplant, cut into chunks
1¾ cups canned full-fat coconut milk (or see page 180 for coconut milk recipe)
2 cups chicken stock/bone broth or vedge stock (see pages 136 and 140)
6 kaffir lime leaves
7 ounces fine green beans, topped and halved
½ bunch of fresh Thai basil
2 limes, cut into wedges
Sea salt and freshly ground black pepper

To make the paste, put the garlic, shallots, ginger, lemongrass, galangal, and chiles into a food processor, along with the cumin, ground coriander, black pepper, and half the cilantro. Blitz until finely chopped, add the fish sauce, and blitz again until you have a rough paste.

To make the curry using butternut squash, steam the chunks until just tender, then quickly pan-fry in ghee for 1-2 minutes, or until the outer edges take on a little golden color. Remove from the pan to a plate. If using chicken, slice the meat into 1-inch strips, and put into a large pan over medium heat with 1 tablespoon of ghee. Fry for 5-7 minutes, turning the strips, until just turning golden, then transfer to a plate.

Return the pan to medium heat, add the mushrooms and eggplant, and fry for 4-5 minutes, or until golden. Try not to stir them too much, and cook in a single layer. Transfer to a plate.

Reduce the heat to medium-low and add the paste for 4-5 minutes, stirring occasionally. Pour in the coconut milk, and the broth or stock, and add the lime leaves. Increase the heat, and bring gently to a boil, then simmer for 10 minutes, or until reduced slightly.

Stir in the butternut squash or chicken, and mushrooms, reduce the heat to low and cook for an additional 5 minutes, or until the chicken is cooked through, adding the beans for the final 3 minutes.

Season carefully to taste. Pick, roughly chop and stir through the basil leaves and remaining cilantro leaves. Serve with lime wedges and steamed rice or cauliflower rice (see page 49).

A few crazy good finishing salts.

Not only is salt is essential to the body, but when paired with other bits and pieces, dried herbs and ends of things that usually go in the garbage, it can be a crazy good seasoning. Iodized table salt is no good, though—you must use good-quality salt, so be prepared to pay more. Not only is iodized table salt bad for your health, it's just too salty, and has a horrid aftertaste. Flaky sea salt, rock salt, pink Himalayan salt, and the lovely, moist grayish toned French salts are all good for you, and have slightly different mineral and flavor compositions. Quality salt is also known to help preserve two feel-good hormones in the body—serotonin and melatonin—which help us to sleep, relax, and feel good. What more do I need to say? Except: Pass the salt!

FOR THE BASE
¼ cup flaky sea salt—rock salt (ground) or pink
   Himalayan salt

Sumac and sesame salt: Great with pumpkin soup, avocado on toast, roast veggies, and chicken.

Add 2 teaspoons of sumac and 1 tablespoon of toasted sesame seeds to the salt, and grind to a fine powder using a mortar and pestle.

Celery salt: Perfect with soft-boiled eggs, quails' eggs, avocado, soup, and roast veggies.

Toast the leaves from the head of 1 bunch of celery (no stalks) in a dry skillet until crisp with no moisture left. Add to the sea salt, and grind to an emerald green powder using a mortar and pestle.

Kale ash salt: Amazing on almost anything—pasta, salads, avocado, roast squash, beets, and eggs.

Add 2 tablespoons of kale ash (see page 104) to the sea salt, and grind to a fine powder using a mortar and pestle.

Cumin salt: Delicious sprinkled over roast beets, avocado, roast squash, lamb, chicken, scrambled eggs, and omelets.

Toast 2 tablespoons of cumin seeds in a dry skillet until fragrant and slightly darker in color. Add to the salt, and grind to a fine powder using a mortar and pestle.

Hibiscus salt: Try with lamb, avocado, stews, and casseroles.

Add 1 tablespoon of dried hibiscus flowers to the sea salt, and grind to a fine powder using a mortar and pestle.

Flower salt: Stunning over roast chicken, fresh mozzarella, and salads.

Grind the salt to a fine powder using a mortar and pestle, then add 1 teaspoon of dried Damascan rose petals, 1 teaspoon of dried cornflowers, and 1 teaspoon of dried calendula petals. Grind again, just enough to break up the petals, but not too much.

Homemade butter: the original superfood.

MAKES JUST UNDER 2¼ POUNDS BUTTER
AND ABOUT 1 QUART BUTTERMILK

Butter is one of my favorite things in the world! Eating it spread thickly on homemade sourdough bread straight out of the oven makes me as happy as can be.

Butter used to be considered unhealthy because it contains saturated fat. That, however, is not a valid argument against eating butter, because the saturated fat myth has been thoroughly debunked in recent years. When butter comes from lovely healthy grass-fed cows, it is one of nature's most precious foods. It is packed full of heart-healthy fats, which nourish the brain and give instant energy to the body. Putting a knob of butter on your cooked veggies allows you to absorb all the fat-soluble vitamins that are present in the vegetables, whereas if you eat vegetables without healthy fats, you only get benefit from some of the nutrients.

Butter is also jam-packed with heart-healthy fats such as vitamin K2 to support bone density; Vitamin A, which helps to maintain thyroid, adrenal, and cardiovascular health, and along with vitamins D and E, is a key antioxidant; omega-3 fatty acids, conjugated linoleic acid (CLA), which helps reduce belly fat, protects against cancer and encourages muscle growth.

There are now plenty of good-quality organic grass-fed butters available in the supermarkets, and some even sell unpasteurized butter. However, nothing is more satisfying than making your own. It's easy, and well worth the effort. Get the kids involved too—they'll love it.

Unsalted butter should be eaten within a few days, but salted butter lasts for a couple of weeks.

For this method, your best bet is to use a pair of butter pats to make it easier to shape the final butter into blocks. If you don't have any butter pats, just use your hands.

Sunlight taints butter, so if serving it outdoors, try to keep it covered. When storing the butter, keep it in a covered butter dish.

8½ cups organic heavy cream, at room temperature (unpasteurized or pasteurized, but make sure it is not homogenized)

1½ teaspoons sea salt flakes—omit if you want unsalted butter, or to make ghee

Soak your wooden butter pats in ice water for 30 minutes, so that they will stick less to the butter when shaping it.

Pour the cream into a sterilized, chilled mixing bowl and whisk at medium speed. It will undergo various stages— softly whipped, then stiffly whipped, then it will start to collapse and separate. You will see the buttermilk start sloshing around the bowl: keep going until it is well separated. Pour into a spotlessly clean strainer set over a bowl, and allow the buttermilk to drain from the butter.

Put the butter back into a clean bowl, and beat with a whisk for an additional 30 seconds to 1 minute to expel any remaining buttermilk. Remove, and drain through the strainer as before. (Keep the buttermilk in the fridge ready to use in other recipes.)

Fill the bowl containing the butter with ice water. Using the butter pats or your hands, knead the butter to force out any remaining buttermilk. Do not be tempted to skip this step, as any buttermilk remaining in the butter will sour, and cause the butter to go off. If you handle the butter too much with your hands, it will liquify, so act quickly for this stage. Drain the water, and repeat a couple more times, or until the water is totally clear, and you are sure there is no more buttermilk.

To salt the entire batch, spread the butter out thinly, sprinkle with the salt and massage it in with wet hands. To make only some of it salted, divide the butter into blocks and add a couple of pinches of salt for every 4 ounces or so of butter.

Pat the butter into separate portions using the soaked butter pats, or your wet hands. If you find the butter is still sticking, try shaping it in the ice water. Wrap in waxed paper, and store in the fridge.

A basic nut butter.

MAKES 1 JAM JAR

Nut butter is one of my obsessions. It is amazing on a surprisingly large amount of things. Including porridge. Yes, you heard that right. A quick snack that my son loves, is an old classic: nut butter spread on a crisp and crunchy celery stick, or sometimes a slice of crisp apple. I also love it with fresh paleo bread (see page 157) on top of a generous spread of butter, and topped with a drizzle of raw honey. Nuts that work well in nut butters are almonds, cashews, pecans, walnuts, brazil nuts, and macadamias. You can also mix the nuts up if you like, and you could even add sunflower or pumpkin seeds.

14 ounces nuts, soaked overnight, then roasted at a low temperature, or dehydrated until crispy	A pinch of sea salt 1–2 tablespoons coconut oil

Tip: You can roast the nuts beforehand to create a slightly different flavor. Roasted almonds make great butter, as do roasted cashews and roasted pecans.

Tip: For a sweet nut butter, add 1 tablespoon of raw honey.

Place the nuts in a food processor. Blend for 5 minutes, scraping down the sides of the bowl if necessary. Add a generous pinch of sea salt and the coconut oil (I usually find 1 tablespoon is enough, but it depends on the nuts). Blitz again. At this point, you should have a lovely, creamy nut butter.

Scrape into a glass jar and store in the pantry. The nut butter will last for at least 6-8 weeks if stored in a cool place away from the light. It's delicious with my spiced almond and coconut bread on page 157.

Coconut butter.

MAKES 1 SMALL JAR

You can use this in place of butter on bread, or when baking. It's absolutely delicious and lasts well. A spoon or two added to smoothies helps with feelings of satiety and weight loss, due to its metabolism-boosting qualities.

7 ounces coconut flakes

Place the coconut flakes into a food processor or high-speed blender. Start by pulsing, then turn up the power and blitz until you have butter, scraping down the sides of the bowl with a spatula if necessary. The process will take 10–20 minutes in total. It's quicker in a food processor, so do use that if you have one. Store in a glass jar in the pantry.

Herb-flavored butters.

MAKES 9 OUNCES

Fresh herb butters are wonderful with an array of ingredients, and are a handy way to add another flavor dimension to the simplest of dishes. Wild garlic (ramson/ramps) butter is a favorite of mine, as is nasturtium butter, so I tend to make those the most, but all herby butters are delicious. Wild garlic is only around for a short time in the spring, so I love to make this butter, and pop it in the freezer for later use throughout the spring and summer months. (You can do the same with wild garlic oil—see page 119.) It's potent stuff and you don't need much. Wild garlic has a different garlickyness; unlike garlic cloves, it has a deliciously distinctive fresh greenness to it.

You can make other herb butters using different fresh green herbs. Parsley, basil, oregano, chives, rosemary, fennel, dill, and thyme all work well—or try a mixture. Make sure your herbs are completely dry before making the butter because wet herbs make for a soggy butter.

You can make cultured herby butter with the following recipe ideas—simply substitute the butter for my cultured Kefir butter on page 122, and add your favorite herbs from below.

HERB BUTTER

9 ounces salted or
  unsalted butter,
  softened
4 tablespoons finely
  chopped flat-leaf
  parsley, or a mix of
  fresh, soft green herbs

Waxed paper, for
  wrapping

Put the entire butter block into a mixing bowl and mash it up with a fork. When it yields and is soft, add the parsley and mix well.

Tear off a good 12 inches from a roll of waxed paper.

Spoon on half the butter into a log shape. Then roll it up and twist the ends in opposite directions. This will push it together and neaten up the roll. Repeat with the second half, and pop both rolls in the fridge to cool and set. When you are ready to use the butter, slice off wedges as needed, discarding the paper, or unwrap and slice into portions.

Other flavored butters:

Nasturtium butter: Delicious over a piece of freshly pan-fried fish, toasted sourdough bread, and steamed or roasted veggies.
Omit the parsley, and add 7 tablespoons of chopped red, yellow, and golden nasturtium flowers.

Garlic or wild garlic (ramson/ramps) butter: Excellent with fresh baked bread, lamb, fish, beef, chicken, pasta, and steamed or roasted veggies.
Omit the parsley, and add either 6–7 cloves of finely chopped or minced garlic, or 4 tablespoons of finely chopped wild garlic (ramson/ramps) leaves.

Watercress or dill and fennel butter: Beautiful with fish or chicken, or spread on toasted sourdough bread, and topped with avocado, or over steamed or roast veggies.
Omit the parsley, and replace with 4 tablespoons of finely chopped watercress, or 4 tablespoons of finely chopped dill and fennel fronds.

Golden glorious ghee.

MAKES JUST UNDER 2¼ POUNDS

Ghee is food from the gods—liquid gold. It is lactose-free, so even people with a dairy intolerance can have it, providing you're very careful to strain off ALL the milk solids. Ghee is so simple to make, and much cheaper than buying it. It tastes better fresh, too, and it lasts for a very long time, which is why the recipe here is for a big batch.

Although ghee doesn't have to be stored in the fridge, do keep it away from the light, and use a clean utensil each time you dip into the jar. If your kitchen is very warm, you may want to keep it in the fridge as it will last longer. Ghee stored in the fridge will become very solid, which is fine—just scoop out a spoonful as you need it. I use ghee in lots of recipes in the book, as I prefer it to olive oil; ghee has a much higher smoke point, so it doesn't burn easily when you are roasting or pan-frying at high temperatures. Good fats, like ghee, that are correctly prepared and cooked with, are essential to good health, helping the body to make fat-soluble vitamins in our food become available to the body. In Ayurvedic medicine, ghee is known for its healing qualities, and is used internally and externally.

2¼ pounds unsalted butter (you can use more or less; the method and cooking times are pretty much the same)

Line a strainer with paper towels and set over a 2-quart clean glass jar.

Gently melt the butter in a saucepan over medium heat. Once melted, in only a few minutes the butter will separate into three layers: foam will appear as the top layer, the milk solids will migrate to the bottom of the pan, and clarified butter will float between the two.

The foam will gradually die down, then, slowly, bigger bubbles will start to appear, then it will foam again. When the second foam forms, it is ready. This should take 10–15 minutes, depending on how hot you have it.

When you see the second foam, remove the pan from the heat, and allow it to cool a little, and the milk solids to settle at the bottom—do not stir it at any point during the process. Scoop off the top layer of foam using a small double-mesh strainer.

Next, carefully pour the golden central layer through the lined strainer into the jar, leaving the milk solids in the bottom of the pan. If you have succeeded in keeping all the milk solids out of the ghee, and use clean dry utensils each time you dip into the jar, ghee will keep at room temperature for weeks—even months in cooler weather. It can be used as a cooking oil or finishing element, and is also a traditional Ayurvedic body moisturizer.

Chilled flavored olive oils.

MAKES ABOUT 1 CUP

Chilled flavored oils are much the same as the flavored herb butters, but this version is dairy-free, and the olive oil lends its own distinctive flavor. You must chill these oils for them to work properly. During the chilling process the oil becomes solid, which lends its own unique texture and mouthfeel. These chilled oils are great spooned over fish, chicken, pork, lamb, or beef. They are also amazing over my quick greens (see page 48), or over roast or steamed veggies. They will transform your simple fillet of fish (or anything else you choose to put it on) into something supremely amazing.

The oils will last up to a week in the fridge. If you want them to last longer, store them in the freezer in small portions. You could even freeze them in ice cube trays for single portions.

Emerald green herb oil: Works well with beef, chicken, lamb, fish, greens, squash.

HERBS TO CHOOSE FROM	
Thyme, rosemary, parsley, chives, oregano—you can pick a single herb or a combination	2 ounces of your chosen fresh herb(s) 1 cup extra virgin olive oil

Wash and dry the herbs, then lay them flat on a tray lined with a dishtowel, to air-dry completely. When the herbs are completely dry, finely chop them and mix into the olive oil. Refrigerate in a jar with a tight-fitting lid until ready to use.

Ruby red paprika oil: Works well with chicken, lamb, fish, autumn veggies.

2 tablespoons of Spanish paprika, smoked or unsmoked	1 cup extra virgin olive oil 2 garlic cloves, finely minced

Place the paprika in a bowl, and stir in the oil.

Add the garlic, allow it to infuse for 30 minutes, then strain the ruby oil through a fine strainer. Pop in the fridge in a jar with a tight-fitting lid.

Liquid gold, turmeric and ginger oil: Works well with chicken, fish, squash, Asian noodle dishes, shiitake mushrooms, and hearty winter vedge soups.

2 tablespoons of ground turmeric 1 cup extra virgin olive oil	1 teaspoon of freshly grated ginger, plus all the juice A few twists of freshly ground black pepper

Pop the turmeric into a small bowl. Add the oil, ginger, and black pepper. Allow the mix to infuse for 30 minutes before straining. Pour the golden oil into a jar with a tight-fitting lid, and pop into the fridge.

A soft green herb drizzle oil.

MAKES ABOUT ¾ CUP

Basil, wild garlic (ramson/ramps), parsley, tarragon, mint, and dill would work best in this heavenly drizzle oil. Not all together. You want a kind of sludgy verdant sauce that lends a freshness and vibrancy to the dish that you drizzle it over. It has a clean punchy flavor that can really make a dish sing. It is wonderful drizzled over colorful roast autumn squash and heritage beets, roasted baby carrots in the height of spring; it is great over creamy buffalo mozzarella, and double-podded fava beans, and it is also delicious with fish and chicken, and drizzled over soups. It is also amazing drizzled over poached eggs, and avocado on toast. Of course, if you struggle to use it all up, you can add the last bit back to the blender and add some toasted nuts, Parmesan cheese, and lemon juice, and you have pesto. Dill works very well with fish, and tarragon goes beautifully with chicken; mint goes beautifully with lamb, and all the other herbs go with pretty much everything.

2 large handfuls of your choice of fresh, soft green herbs* (you can combine herbs, to complement what you are cooking, or keep it pure and simple by just choosing one herb)
*Basil
*Parsley
*Wild garlic
*Mint
*Tarragon
*Dill
1 fat garlic clove
Sea salt and freshly ground black pepper
¾ cup extra virgin olive oil

Discard the herb stalks and pop the leaves into a high-powered blender or food processor. Add the remaining ingredients and blitz until you have a beautiful moss-green purée. Allow the mix to stand for 1–2 minutes before transferring into a jar with a tight-fitting lid. Refrigerate until ready to use. This oil will keep for up to a few days.

It's all about the kefir.

MAKES 2 CUPS

Kefir is a fermented milk drink. The name comes from the Turkish word *keif*, meaning "good feeling", which aptly describes the benefit of drinking this wonderful beverage. It contains high levels of vitamin B12, calcium, magnesium, vitamin K2, biotin, folate, enzymes, and probiotics, making it one of the most nutritious things you can consume. It has over 20 times the amount of probiotics contained in yogurt, and has been known to help boost immunity, assist in the healing of inflammatory bowel disease, build bone density, fight allergies, improve lactose digestion, kill candida, and assist detoxification. It is also full of healthy fats.

Kefir grains are a natural culture that you can buy in health-food stores and online—or you can get a "starter" from a friend who has already begun to make kefir. The little creamy-colored grains are not, in fact, grains, but cultures of yeast and lactic acid bacteria. When added to milk and left for 24 hours, the microorganisms in the grains multiply and ferment the sugars in the milk, turning it into kefir. The grains are then removed from the thickened liquid, and can be used again to make further batches.

Kefir can be made using the milk from cows, sheep, goats, and also coconut milk. The method is the same whether you use dairy or coconut milk, although if you are making coconut kefir, you need to make a batch of dairy milk kefir every 6–8 batches to keep the grains producing. Remarkably, another benefit of drinking kefir, is that the little grains feed off the lactose in the dairy milk, so by the time it's ready, almost no lactose remains in the kefir, which is great for people who are sensitive to lactose. The coconut kefir, of course, is completely lactose-free. Milk kefir has the consistency of buttermilk. It's quite sour, and a little fizzy and tangy.

Once you have a batch underway, you can ferment it for the recommended time, then strain and use as it is, or you can also do a second ferment to add a secondary flavor (see page 125). Kefir is amazing in smoothies, soups, sauces, homemade ice cream, baking, and marinades. You can make soft kefir cheese from the curds, use the whey to make lacto pickles and bake bread with it. Order some of these miracle grains today, roll up your sleeves, and get involved. You will love it, I promise.

EQUIPMENT
2 x 1 pint glass jars, sterilized (see page 79)
1 plastic-mesh strainer (you can't use a metal one)
1 wooden or plastic spoon (not metal)

TO MAKE THE KEFIR
2 tablespoons milk kefir grains
2 cups non-homogenized whole milk, preferably raw and organic if you can find it, or coconut milk

Pop the milk kefir grains into one of the jars, and pour over the milk. Give the mix a good stir with a wooden spoon and then either place a circle of parchment paper over the top, and secure it with a rubber band, or screw the lid onto the jar.

Allow the kefir to ferment for 12–36 hours on your worktop. Giving it a good shake or stir a couple of times during the fermenting process helps to keep the mix evenly fermenting, and seems to speed up the process a little.

Once the kefir starts to separate, that's a sign it is ready—even a bit over-ready. At this point, just strain off the grains using the plastic strainer, decanting the kefir itself into a new jar, and store in the fridge until you are ready to use it. You can now make a second batch with the strained grains (there's no need to clean them) using the second sterilized jar.

Depending on the warmth of your kitchen, kefir can ferment quite quickly. This is not a problem; it will just make the taste a bit more sour. I like to leave mine for 24 hours, but you can ferment for less time or longer, depending on the level of sourness you prefer.

If your kitchen is warm, your kefir grains will multiply quite quickly—this is a sign that they are healthy, but the more grains to milk you have, the quicker the milk will ferment. If you find it is fermenting too fast, just remove some of the grains when you next strain the kefir, and give them away to your friends, or you can freeze them for later use in case you accidentally kill the ones you have on the worktop. If you forget about your kefir, and leave it for over ten days, it can die off. If this happens, you will need to start again, so it's worth keeping some in the freezer.

My family is quite small, so I don't always use a lot of kefir every day, and sometimes, to slow the fermentation down, I put the strained grains into a clean jar with fresh milk, and then sit the jar in the fridge. The cool temperature of the fridge slows down the process, and the grains can ferment like this for up to a week before you need to strain them, and give them fresh milk. The milk that has fermented in the fridge is perfectly safe, and good to use.

If you want to make a big batch of kefir, bigger than what your grains would ordinarily be able to ferment, you can achieve this with a clever little trick. Simply pop 2-3 tablespoons of kefir grains in a sterilized 2-quart glass jar and add 2-3 cups milk. Cover the jar, and let it ferment for a good 12 hours, stirring occasionally, then top up the milk with an extra 1-1^1/$_2$ quarts of room temperature milk. The kefir you fermented first will act as a starter culture for the extra milk added, and the whole lot will be done in the normal 24-36 hour time frame. Making a big batch this way is handy if you want to make kefir cheese (see page 124), or if you have guests.

When making kefir for the first time, your grains will take some time to adjust to their new home and the new milk, so just be patient; you may need to make a few batches before they really kick into gear, and start working at top speed.

Some people with a low level of healthy bacteria in their gut can experience "die off" symptoms when they start taking kefir. This means that the kefir with all its good bacteria is killing off the high levels of bad bacteria within the gut. If this happens to you, it might not feel that great at first, but it is indeed a wonderful thing, as you are getting your gut bacteria levels back in balance. It is for

this reason that it is advised to start with small amounts of kefir when first introducing it to your diet. If you are not sure if you have low "good" bacteria levels in your gut, just start slowly anyway, and see how you feel. As a general rule, start with 1 teaspoon a day, and keep increasing the dose as long as you feel fine. If you feel any "die off" symptoms, stick to the same level until the die off recedes, and then gradually up the dose again, until you are able to consume as much as you like in your smoothies and whatever else you want to put your kefir into.

Kefir cream.
MAKES 2 CUPS

This cultured cream is heavenly, soft, and delicious, with a lovely tang. You can use it as you would ordinary cream, or you can take it one step further, and make cultured kefir butter.

The fermenting process increases the amounts of immune-boosting probiotics in the cream, lowers levels of lactose, and gives it extra flavor. It lasts well in the fridge, and goes with all sorts of things. I love adding a little raw honey and chopped stem ginger to a small bowl of kefir cream. It's really good!

EQUIPMENT
1 plastic mesh strainer
2 x 1 pint glass jars
(or ceramic bowls),
sterilized (see page 79)
1 wooden or plastic spoon

2–3 tablespoons milk kefir
grains
2 cups heavy cream (or
whipping cream)

Place the kefir grains in one of the glass jars, pour over the cream, give a gentle stir to mix the cream with the grains, cover, and set aside on the worktop for 12–36 hours to ferment—I find 24 hours ideal in the temperature of my kitchen. If your kitchen is cool, it may take up to 36 hours, but if your kitchen is warm it can take as little as 12 hours, so taste it often to see how you like the flavor.

When the fermenting cream is to your desired taste, set the plastic strainer over a bowl and push the cream through it using the spoon, leaving the kefir grains in the strainer.

Pop the kefir grains into the second clean glass jar or bowl to make your next batch, or try the milk kefir, or coconut milk kefir on page 125.

I find that if I use heavy cream, by the time the cream has fermented, it's the perfect softly peaking consistency to use just as it is for decorating cakes, and serving with scones, but if it's too thin, gently whip it, until you have the desired consistency. Store in a glass jar or ceramic bowl in the fridge until you are ready to use it.

If you are using the cream to decorate cakes, add a little coconut sugar, raw honey, or maple syrup to sweeten. Be sure to sweeten the cream before you whip it.

Kefir butter.
MAKES 1 POUND BUTTER AND 2 CUPS CULTURED BUTTERMILK

In recent years I have seen some of my absolute favorite chefs, including Skye Gyngell, use kefir butter in their restaurants. Cultured butter has a very distinctive flavor, and is full of added nutrients. It's not a butter I would use for everyday eating, but it is an amazing treat for a special occasion. Freshly baked homemade sourdough bread with kefir butter is an out-of-this-world start to a very special meal. You could also use this to make herbed kefir butter (see page 114).

EQUIPMENT
1 pair of butter pats

1 quart kefir cream
(see left)
1 teaspoon sea salt, not
too coarse

Follow the method for the plain butter on page 112 and store the kefir butter in the fridge until ready to use.

Kefir cheese.

MAKES 10-14 OUNCES

Kefir cheese is a lovely soft cheese that can be eaten plain, if you like its sour taste, or with added fresh herbs, olive oil, and garlic. It's delicious served alongside salads, roast vegetables, or eaten with my Spiced almond crackers (see page 157) or crudités.

The thickness of your kefir will determine how much cheese you get. The thinner the kefir, the less cheese it will yield.

Because the fermenting process removes almost all the lactose, people who are lactose intolerant can enjoy this, and benefit from all the probiotics and vitamins it contains. It's very easy to make, and is a great way of using up surplus kefir. When you make this cheese, a lot of whey is produced, but it doesn't go to waste—see the tips below for ways to use it.

EQUIPMENT
Plastic-mesh strainer
Large cheesecloth, doubled over
Large bowl

TO MAKE THE KEFIR CHEESE
3⅓ cups milk kefir (see page 120)

TO FLAVOR THE CHEESE (optional)
A handful of finely chopped fresh soft herbs, such as dill, parsley, and chives
A glug of extra virgin olive oil
1 garlic clove, finely grated or mashed
Sea salt and freshly ground black pepper

Use the cheesecloth to line the strainer in a double layer hanging over the sides, and place over a large bowl. Pour the kefir into the lined strainer, then gather up the sides of the cheesecloth, and tie them together tightly with a long piece of string.

Suspend the cheesecloth with the kefir in it over the bowl, by tying it in a position where it can hang, so that the whey drips into the bowl. (I often hang my cheesecloth bag on one of my cupboard handles with the bowl underneath.)

Leave for at least 5–6 hours or overnight—the whey will continue to drip into the bowl. If you like your kefir cheese thicker, just leave it for longer—anywhere up to 24 hours. If it has stopped dripping, it is probably fully drained, in which case it is ready.

Unwrap the cheese, and pour the whey into a clean glass jar, and store in the fridge for later use. You can leave the kefir cheese plain, or tip it into a bowl and mix in the flavorings. The cheese will last well for up to 10 days in the fridge.

If the kefir is dripping through the cheesecloth, not just the clear-ish whey, but the milky white kefir too, you may need to make a triple layer of cheesecloth in place of the double. It depends on how fine your cheesecloth is.

Leftover whey can be used to soak/activate grains, nuts, and seeds. If you don't have time to use the whey immediately, simply pop it in the freezer until you need it.

Whey can also be added to lacto-fermented veggies as a starter culture. The whey is full of good bacteria, which prevent the growth of bad bacteria, and speed up the fermenting process.

Kefir: a second ferment.

MAKES 2 CUPS

Kefir is great on its own, added to smoothies, or used to cook with, or you can create a second ferment. This is very easy to do, and gives tasty results. If I'm adding kefir to smoothies, I keep it plain, but if I want to drink it as it is, or use as a yogurt to serve with fruit, I like to flavor it as per below. No kefir grains are required for this recipe.

FOR THE BASE
2 cups ready-made kefir
  (you can use coconut
  milk or animal milk)

FOR THE FLAVORS:

Hibiscus and rose.
Add 1 tablespoon of dried hibiscus flowers and 1 teaspoon of rose water to a 1-pint jar of ready-made kefir, and stir. Cover, and leave to ferment on the worktop for 12–24 hours, stirring occasionally. Strain out the hibiscus flowers, stir in 2–3 tablespoons of maple syrup, and pour the flavored kefir into a clean jar. Keep in the fridge until ready to use.

Vanilla and raw honey.
Add 1 vanilla bean, seeds scraped out and the bean, to a 1-pint jar of ready-made kefir. Cover, and leave to ferment on the worktop for 12 hours. Add 2–3 tablespoons of raw honey, stir, and then pop in the fridge until ready to use.

Orange and cardamom.
Add the seeds from 2 cardamom pods (whole pods lightly toasted in a dry skillet, then crushed to a fine powder) and 1 teaspoon of orange blossom water, or 2 thumb-sized pieces of orange peel to a 1-pint jar of ready-made kefir. Cover, and leave to ferment on the worktop for 12 hours or overnight, then add 2 tablespoons of raw honey, stir, and refrigerate until ready to use.

Coconut milk kefir.

MAKES 2 CUPS

Coconut milk makes delicious kefir—thick, creamy, and tasting just like coconut yogurt at a fraction of the price, and in nutritional terms, it's even better for you, as it contains over 20 times more probiotics. You can use canned coconut milk or make your own (see page 180); either way, be sure to use full fat—coconut fat is extremely good for you. Your kefir will set a bit in the fridge as the coconut fat hardens on cooling, but just give the kefir a bit of a stir when you bring it out of the fridge, and it will very quickly become creamy again. Coconut kefir is a lot thicker than dairy milk kefir, which is why I tend to make it more often, because I like to use it instead of yogurt to have with my fruit in the morning. I find cow's milk kefir, being thinner, is good for making cheese and adding to smoothies, while coconut kefir is good to use in place of yogurt.

EQUIPMENT
2 1-pint glass jars,
  sterilized (see page 79)
Plastic-mesh strainer
Wooden or plastic spoon
  (not metal)

2 tablespoons milk kefir
  grains
1¾ cups full-fat coconut
  milk

Put the kefir grains into one of the glass jars, pour over the coconut milk, stir well, then cover, and leave to ferment on the worktop for 24–36 hours. When your kefir is to your desired taste, strain through the strainer into the second clean jar, and it is ready for use. Wash the original jar, pop the strained grains back into it, and start again with another batch.

Store the coconut kefir in the fridge until you are ready to use it. It will keep in the fridge for at least one week, if not two.

Homemade creamy yogurt

MAKES ABOUT 3⅓ CUPS

This is the easiest way I have found to make yogurt at home without special equipment or warming drawers, or strange additives. It makes a delicious, very creamy yogurt, perfect for using in all manner of ways. I like to use raw organic milk, but that can be hard to find and expensive; the next best thing is to use organic whole milk that has not been homogenized.

EQUIPMENT
Digital thermometer
1-quart Thermos bottle, cleaned
    with boiling water to sterilize it

4 heaping tablespoons organic
    thick, plain, live yogurt
2¾ cups organic whole milk
⅔ cup light cream
4½ tablespoons milk powder
    (optional)
1 probiotic capsule (contents only,
    capsule discarded)

Start by placing the yogurt into a perfectly clean and dry glass or ceramic bowl, and allow it to come up to room temperature; this will take about 30 minutes.

Next place a medium saucepan over low heat, and pour in the milk and cream. Stir until it reaches exactly 114.8°F on your digital thermometer, not one degree more (if it gets hotter than this, it will kill all the live cultures in the yogurt when it is poured over it). Remove the pan from the heat, and sprinkle in the milk powder, if using, whisking to combine. Set aside to cool for 2–3 minutes, no more.

Add the contents of the probiotics capsule and whisk again. Carefully pour the milk mixture onto the yogurt, and gently stir to thoroughly combine. Pour the mixture into the Thermos, and screw the lid on as tight as you can. Leave the bottle on the worktop overnight.

In the morning you should have lovely thick yogurt in your bottle. Pour the yogurt into a glass jar or ceramic bowl with a lid, and transfer to the fridge. Best eaten within five to six days.

To make little creamy fruit and yogurt pots, simply spoon some seasonal fruit compote into a small pot with a lid, filling about one-third of the pot, then spoon over your plain homemade yogurt to fill the pot. If you like, you can sweeten the yogurt with a little raw honey or maple syrup before spooning it on top of the fruit. These make great snacks for kids or adults alike as part of a healthy lunchbox or casual after-dinner treat.

Cashew yogurt
(cashew-gurt)

MAKES 1 PINT JAR

This stuff is seriously smooth, creamy, and decadent. It has a distinct flavor of cashews and is quite different from dairy or coconut yogurt, much richer and creamier—more luscious, I would say. It still has that lovely distinctive yogurt tang because it is lightly fermented. The fermentation process adds a plentiful amount of immune-boosting probiotics, and of course, it is lactose-free. I love to add vanilla as here, but you can also keep it plain, and that means you can use it for both sweet and savory dishes. The sweet version is great to have with fruit for breakfast or on top of puddings for dessert. The yogurt works best if you blend the nuts with a high-speed blender. It still works just as well with a regular blender, but it won't be as smooth. The texture of cashew yogurt is slightly different from cow's milk yogurt or coconut yogurt: it's more pourable, and doesn't set into curds, but is equally delicious in a nutty-creamy kind of way.

EQUIPMENT
Sterilized glass jar (see page 79)

1 heaping cup raw cashews, soaked
    for at least 4 hours or overnight
1 tablespoon lemon juice
A pinch of fine sea salt
1 scant cup filtered water, more
    if needed

1 probiotic capsule (contents only,
    capsule discarded)

FOR A SWEET VERSION (optional)
1 vanilla bean, split lengthwise,
    seeds scraped out and reserved
2 teaspoons raw honey, maple
    syrup, or stevia

Drain and rinse the cashews, then put them in a blender along with the other ingredients, and blitz for several minutes until you have a completely smooth paste. If you want a sweet version, add the vanilla seeds and sweetener of choice, and blitz again to incorporate.

Pour the cashew mix into the jar and cover with a breathable material, such as a linen napkin or waxed paper with knife slits in it. Wrap a rubber band around the mouth of the jar to keep the cover secure. Place the cashew-gurt somewhere warm and dry to ferment for 6–24 hours or up to 36 hours, depending on the temperature of your room. The cashew-gurt is ready when tiny bubbles start to appear, and it has a lovely tangy, sour taste. Replace the cover with a secure lid, and refrigerate until ready to eat.

Tip: If you live in a very hot or humid climate, you will only need to culture the yogurt for 5–6 hours as the warm temperature in your kitchen will speed up the culturing process very fast.

Coconut yogurt.
MAKES ABOUT 2 CUPS

This delightfully creamy and smooth yogurt is a great alternative to dairy yogurt. When I have tropical fruits for breakfast, I prefer to enjoy them with coconut yogurt rather than cow's milk yogurt—the flavors just work better.

Most commercial brands of coconut yogurt are thickened with tapioca starch, which is not great for anyone with digestive issues, as it can cause havoc in the gut. Making your own is a great way to get all the coconut goodness, and none of the nasty thickeners.

---

3 14-ounce cans full-fat (and additive-free) coconut milk, chilled upside down in the fridge overnight

2 capsules of probiotics (contents only, capsules discarded)

Take the coconut milk out of the fridge, turn the cans the right way up, and open. Carefully drain off the thin liquid that forms at the top into a bowl and reserve.

What remains in each can is the hardened coconut fat, which you can spoon out into a separate clean bowl.

Using a whisk or hand-held electric beaters, whip the solid coconut fat into a soft cream. This should only take 1–2 minutes. If it's too thick, you can add a dash of the reserved milk to loosen the mix.

When the coconut cream has a lovely soft consistency of whipped cream, pour it into a glass jar and add the contents of the probiotic capsules, stir with a wooden spoon, then cover the jar with a breathable lid such as a paper towel fastened in place with a rubber band.

Set the jar in a warm place to ferment. The linen cupboard is great, or a warm spot in the kitchen. Leave for 24–36 hours. Taste it after 12–24 hours to see if it has reached your desired level of tangy sourness. Little bubbles will start to appear, which will tell you it is ready .

Remove the cover, replace with a tight-fitting lid, and transfer to the fridge. It will last for about 10 days if kept cool, although it will harden in the fridge. To soften it, simply stir vigorously with a wooden spoon.

Roasted garlic cultured nut cheez
with fresh herbs and cracked pepper.
MAKES A 6-INCH ROUND CHEEZ

This is a cheese of sorts, hence the name "cheez" and not cheese. It's not dairy cheese; it's made from a base of nuts and cultured with probiotics, which makes it great for lactose-intolerant people or anyone who just wants to avoid dairy. Don't expect delicious melty, stinking brie—much as I love it (brie that is!), this is good in its own unique way.

You can leave out the roast garlic if you don't fancy it (personally, I can't get enough) and just keep it as a plain nut cheez with lovely fresh herbs. You could serve it with my crackers on page 157, or crusty fresh sourdough bread or crudités. It will last in the fridge for up to a week.

FOR THE CHEEZ
½–1 small garlic bulb, depending on how garlicky you like your food
2 tablespoons finely chopped thyme and rosemary leaves, plus extra to serve
1 teaspoon freshly cracked pink peppercorns (use black peppercorns if you can't find pink, and crack using a mortar and pestle not a grinder), plus extra to serve
1 cup raw cashews, soaked in water for a minimum of 4 hours or overnight

3½ tablespoons coconut butter (see page 113), or ½ cup unsweetened coconut flakes soaked in hot water for a minimum of 15 minutes, then drained
¼ teaspoon sea salt
3 tablespoons lemon juice
1 probiotic capsule (contents only, capsule discarded)

EQUIPMENT
18-inch square of cheesecloth
6-inch round cake pan or dish
Plastic wrap

Preheat the oven to 350°F.

Start by cutting the top of the garlic off, just enough to expose all the tops of the cloves. Wrap the whole bulb neatly in foil, pop it in the oven, and roast for about 40 minutes, or until fragrant, and the cloves are meltingly tender. Remove from the oven, set aside, and allow to cool completely before moving to the next step.

Line the pan or dish first with plastic wrap, then with the cheesecloth and sprinkle in most of the chopped herbs and pink peppercorns (reserve some to sprinkle on top).

Place the cashews, coconut butter, salt, lemon juice, and the contents of the probiotic capsule into a high-powered blender or food processor. Blitz for a couple of minutes, or until completely smooth. Squeeze the roasted garlic out of its skin and add that too, then blitz again until thoroughly incorporated. You may need to stop the motor, scrape down the sides of the bowl, and blitz again to keep it all smooth and combined.

Scrape the mix into the prepared pan, firming the cheez down into the herbs and cheesecloth. Tap the pan down on the worktop a few times to level it out. Sprinkle with the reserved herbs and crushed pink peppercorns. Next, bring the sides of the cheesecloth up and over so the cheez is totally covered. Place a small plate on top of the cloth and weigh it down with a can of beans or something heavy. Set aside on the worktop for several hours before placing the whole thing, weight and all, into the fridge to set for 24 hours.

The next day, remove the weight, unwrap the cheez, lay a plate over the uncovered cheez and gently flip it over so that the cheez is now on the plate. Remove the cloth completely. Sprinkle with any extra herbs or pepper, and either serve, or keep it in an airtight container in the fridge for up one week.

Labneh

MAKES ABOUT 2 CUPS

Labneh is an easy-to-make soft dripped yogurt, with the consistency of a soft cheese. It is a staple of the Middle East. You can make it from cow's, goat's or sheep's milk yogurt. It's best to use the thicker Greek-style yogurt, as that will give you a higher yield. Labneh can be turned into a savory or sweet dish, you can roll it into balls flavored with fresh herbs and spices, and submerge it in olive oil for a delicious and beautiful snack, or as part of a mezze platter. Sweet or savory, you will love it; it's incredibly easy to make, and super versatile.

EQUIPMENT
1 strainer
1 piece of cheesecloth
1 medium bowl

3½ cups thick, whole milk, or plain Greek yogurt
2 teaspoons sea salt (optional, for the savory version)

Place the yogurt in a medium bowl, and if you are making savory labneh, add the salt, and give it a good stir.

Next, line a strainer with the cheesecloth, and set the strainer over a bowl, allowing the cloth to hang down over the sides. Scrape the yogurt into the cheesecloth-lined strainer. Gather up the sides of the cheesecloth and tie them tightly together with a long piece of string.

Suspend the cheesecloth with the yogurt in it over the bowl by tying it somewhere it can hang, and the whey can drip into the bowl. Leave overnight, and the whey will continue to drip. The next morning you will have labneh. If you would like it thicker, just let it hang for a bit longer, anything up to 24 hours is good. Unwrap the labneh from the cheesecloth, and decant the whey from the bowl into a glass jar or other container.

The labneh will keep in the fridge for three to four days.

You will end up with a bowlful of whey that drips out of the yogurt. Whey is a wonderful thing and can be used in other recipes such as the mung dahl on page 33, in place of stock or water. It's full of protein and tastes great when you cook with it, adding a certain depth of flavor and richness. If you can't use the whey right away, it will keep in the freezer for a good few months.

Labneh balls rolled in Pistachio and kale ash dukkah

1 quantity of Pistachio and kale ash dukkah (see page 104)
2 cups savory Labneh

Sprinkle several tablespoons of the dukkah onto a plate, then take walnut-sized pieces of labneh, roll them into balls and roll the balls in the dukkah. Continue until you have finished all the labneh. You may need to add more dukkah to the plate as you go. Serve these little balls as part of a mezze platter, picnic or with crusty sourdough bread. You could also pack them into jars fully submerged with olive oil—they make great gifts.

Spiced savory labneh balls in olive oil

2 cups savory labneh
1⅔ tablespoons finely chopped fresh thyme leaves
1⅔ tablespoons red pepper flakes

1 teaspoon ground sumac
Zest of 2 unwaxed lemons
About 3 cups extra virgin olive oil

To make these little balls, sprinkle the herbs and spices onto a plate, then take walnut-sized pieces of labneh, roll them into balls, and roll the balls in the herbs and spices. Continue until you have finished all the labneh. Carefully place the balls into a wide-necked 1-quart sterilized glass jar (see page 79) or several little jars, and top up with the olive oil, ensuring the balls are fully submerged. Screw the lids onto the jar(s). The labneh will keep like this for several months in the fridge. Let come to room temperature before enjoying. Once opened, eat within two weeks.

A rich chicken broth.

MAKES ABOUT 4¼ QUARTS

This is the perfect broth: delicious, nourishing, and gelatin rich, which is amazing for skin, joints, healing the gut, reducing inflammation, balancing hormones, and much more. You can drink cups of this just as it is for a restorative gut-healing drink, or you can use it in soups, casseroles, and stews. You can also reduce it right down to make gravies and sauces.

2–3 chicken carcasses
4 prepared chicken feet (optional)
3 tablespoons apple cider vinegar
Filtered or spring water (about
    3–4 quarts, enough to cover
    the bones)
3 large carrots, peeled and chopped
2 large celery stalks, washed and
    chopped

2 large onions, washed and
    quartered (skins can be left on if
    they're organic)
6 garlic cloves, skin on, lightly
    bashed
A handful of parsley, stalks and all
2 bay leaves
2 teaspoons whole black
    peppercorns (no salt—see page
    138)

Put the chicken carcasses (and feet too, if using) in a large pot. Add the vinegar, and enough cold filtered water to cover the bones, with a little extra room to allow for the veggies.

Place over medium heat, and slowly bring to a boil, skimming off any scum that rises to the surface. When most of the scum has gone, and the water is close to boiling, add the veggies, herbs, and peppercorns (no salt!). Return to a gentle simmer, cover with a tight-fitting lid, and reduce the heat to the lowest possible setting. Cook at a bare simmer for a minimum of 6 hours and up to 12, occasionally skimming off any scum that rises to the top.

When the broth has cooked for long enough, remove the bones and pour the broth through a fine-mesh strainer. Allow to cool before transferring to the fridge or freezer.

If you want to defat the stock, allow it to cool in a wide-necked container, then pop in the fridge overnight. In the morning, a layer of solid fat will have formed on the top, which you can simply lift off. Don't throw it away though; use it for roasting or sautéing vegetables.

Nourishing bone broth.

Making bone broth is an incredibly old and nourishing tradition in almost all cultures. Somewhere along the way, some places lost the knowledge and habit of making this truly magical elixir. It has so many health benefits, partly due to the gelatin and collagen that real bone broth contains (unlike broth or stock made from powders or cubes) and the unique combination of amino acids, minerals, and cartilage compounds, which are to be found in the simmering broth. Protein plays a crucial role in pretty much every single biological process within the body, and amino acids are the building blocks of protein. Our cells, muscles, and tissues are made up of a large proportion of amino acids, which makes them essential for our bodies to function in a healthy way. Minerals are important for many reasons too; they help us with building strong bones and teeth, blood, skin, and hair, nerve function, and building muscle. They also help metabolic processors such as those that turn food into energy. Bone broth and meat stocks contain minerals in a form the body can absorb easily—not just calcium, but also magnesium, phosphorus, silicon, sulfur, and trace minerals. Bone broth also contains the broken down material from cartilage and tendons—stuff like chondroitin sulphates, and glucosamine, now sold as expensive supplements for arthritis and joint pain.

Nourishing bone broth will help with speedy recovery from surgery and illness, healing of pain and inflammation anywhere in the body, increasing energy levels from better digestion, lessening of allergies, and assistance in the recovery from autoimmune diseases. It also helps with the recovery of common colds and flu. Mineral- and protein-rich broth can also help reduce cravings of all sorts, due to its nutritional profile, which has an extremely nourishing effect on the body as a whole.

Bone broth is typically simmered for between 6 and 48 hours. Some people with severe digestive and neurological issues cannot tolerate the broth when it has been cooked for this long, due to the profile of amino acids within it. Some people have MSG sensitivities, which long-simmered broth has in its natural form. On various gut-healing diets, such as the GAPS diet and the SCD lifestyle (specific carbohydrate diet), it is advised to start with meat stock, which is similar to broth, but, rather than just bones, whole legs and thighs of chickens are simmered, and it is cooked for a far shorter time, typically anything from 1 to 3 hours for poultry, and up to 6 hours for beef. The meat stock is milder in flavor, and the meat can be eaten when the stock is cooked. It is much gentler than the broth, although both are incredibly healing, nourishing foods. The gelatin present in meat stock and broth is a key superfood for healing a leaky gut, and soothing inflammatory digestive disorders. It protects and heals the mucosal lining of the digestive tract, and helps to regenerate cells. It also aids in the digestion and absorption of nutrients.

Of all the different meats that can be used to make bone broth, fish broth, made from whole fish frames including the head, is the most potent and healing. White fish is best for making fish broth, because the highly unsaturated oils contained in oily fish become rancid during cooking. Other bits of animals that many people in western cultures find hard to cook include chicken feet, and pig's feet—these are the parts that contain the most gelatin. Asian cooks often add these to their broth pots, which makes their broth so full of gelatin, that as it cools in the fridge, it sets like jelly. Over time I have grown used to adding these ingredients to my simmering broth pots; the taste is no different from making the broth without them, but the health benefits are far superior, so I just decided to get used to it. After all, if I can happily eat a steak, why not add a pig's foot to my broth?

To get the most out of your broth, have a read through the following points before you start making broth a regular part of your weekly routine for optimal health.

TIPS FOR MAKING BROTH LIKE A PRO
When broth won't jell...
Ideally, you want to make a broth that jells in the fridge once it is cool. It should set like a soft, wobbly jelly. If your broth doesn't "jell up", you might not have used the right variety of bones—for a delicious and nutritionally balanced broth that

Nourishing bone broth
(continued).

jells well, you want a good mix of bones, and in particular, ones with a lot of cartilage on them which specifically help the broth to jell. One quick way to ensure this, is by adding chicken feet and/or split pig's feet to the broth. As a general rule of thumb, it's best to add the right mix of bones that yield gelatin, and other types of bones that add both flavor and color. Free-range chickens often give better jelling results than regular barn-raised chickens. Many people report that they get better jell using pasture-raised chicken carcasses over conventional chicken carcasses.

Another reason your broth may not have jelled, is that the bones to water ratio was not in balance. You want to only add just enough water to cover the bones. However, if you are simmering broth on the stovetop, you may need to top up with a little extra water, because quite a lot will evaporate during the long cooking time. Cover the pot with a tight-fitting lid to minimize the amount of evaporation. Otherwise, cook the broth slowly in the oven, again with a lid on the pot, so that not much water evaporates.

In addition, broth won't jell if it has been cooked at too high a temperature. Simmer your broth very gently, no hard-and fast-boiling.

Clear or cloudy?

Cloudy broth is just fine as a base for soups, casseroles and stews, but ideally you want it clear for serving as a light soup.

To achieve beautifully clear broth, you need to be careful when it first comes to a boil, scooping off any scum that rises to the surface, and discarding it. Don't let the broth actually boil—as it comes up to temperature and starts to bubble, immediately reduce the heat to a gentle simmer.

Another good tip for keeping broth clear, is to wash and dry the bones before roasting them, and then adding them to the broth pot. Obviously you can't wash and dry a chicken carcass, but big meatless beef bones and lamb bones can easily be washed.

Salt.

The one seasoning that should never be added to broth or stocks is salt. This is because if you want to boil down, or reduce the liquid once it has finished cooking, it will become way too salty. Add salt to your soup, stew, gravy, or sauce at the end of the cooking process when you have reached the desired thickness. When you do add your salt at this final stage, it's best to use lovely pure sea salt, or Himalayan salt, both of which are additive-free and full of essential trace minerals.

Water.

It is best to use clean, filtered water for making broth, because the chemical content in highly fluoridated, and chlorinated water will only become more concentrated as the water evaporates during the cooking. Fluoride and chlorine do not support health, and can have detrimental effects on the gut and digestive system. It's best to use fresh spring water, mineral water, filtered water, rainwater from a tank, or if you're lucky enough, beautiful fresh well water.

Vinegar.

Vinegar helps to extract minerals from the bones and veggies. Small amounts do not change the flavor of the broth, and you don't need to use raw vinegar, as it will be heated during the cooking process, so any good apple cider vinegar will do.

Aromatics

Classic stock calls for the addition of certain vegetables and herbs, traditionally referred to as aromatics. Ideally, these are added after the initial skimming of any scum that rises to the surface, as the broth/stock is hard to skim when there are a lot of vegetables and herbs in the pot.

If you have organic onions, you can leave their skins on to add both flavor and color. When making Vietnamese pho, the onions are often charred before being added to the pot to give an extra layer of flavor—this is well worth a try. Both onions and carrots add sweetness, and celery lends a distinctive savory flavor. As for herbs, the classic addition is a bouquet garni—sprigs of thyme and parsley, plus a fresh bay leaf or two. Peppercorns lend warmth and flavor to the broth. You can add them whole, or crush them. Again, it's best to add them after the initial skimming stage, otherwise you usually end up accidentally skimming off all the peppercorns with the scum if you add them too soon.

Finishing and straining your broth/stock.

Once the broth has finished cooking, use tongs or a slotted spoon to scoop out the bones and veggies, then strain the liquid through a fine-mesh strainer. The broth is now ready to use.

Storage.

Glass is definitely the cheapest and healthiest storage option. The ideal jars for broth or stock must be freezer-safe with wide necks and strong seals. Glass jars are easy to clean and sterilize in the dishwasher, and can be used an infinite number of times. They also do not leach plastics into your food, unlike plastic containers. To ensure they don't explode in the freezer, only fill glass jars three-quarters full, and allow the broth to cool completely before transferring the jars to the freezer. Broth will last quite a while in the fridge—it varies depending on the broth, but they should last at least a few days, and up to a week. If there is a big layer of fat on top which seals off the broth underneath, it can last even longer, up to 10 days or more. As long as your broth smells good and fresh when you heat it up, it will be fine to use.

Make broth a part of your routine.

In recent years I have made broth in my household more and more. It has now become part of my weekly routine. I usually buy a chicken to roast at least once a week, and it always gets turned into a broth. Sometimes I buy chicken carcasses from my local organic supplier, and use them when I don't want the whole chicken. I love having a couple of jars of broth in the freezer for meal emergencies; when the fridge is bare, you can easily whip up a quick dinner with some broth by adding the odd leftover bit of veggies, or a poached egg. Another reason for keeping broth in the fridge, is for when you find yourself really hungry and don't have time to cook—simply heat up a cup of broth. It is so satisfying, and will put an immediate stop to any sugar cravings.

Other uses for broth.

A great way of making grains and pseudo-cereals more digestible, aside from soaking them, is to cook them in broth. I often cook rice and quinoa in broth for my son. He loves the added flavor boost, and they are gentler on his digestive system cooked this way, not to mention all the extra nutrients... win win.

Beef or lamb bone broth.

Beef or lamb broth is super tasty and full of goodness. It's richer than chicken broth, and fuller in flavor. Roasting the bones first really brings out the deep flavors of the beef and lamb. This wonderful broth is essential if you're making any sort of beef or shepherd's pie. Just reduce the broth down to get a more concentrated flavor.

2¼ pounds beef or lamb bones (use bones with plenty of cartilage on them)

Filtered or spring water (about 3–4 quarts, enough to cover the bones)

1 celery stalk, chopped

2 carrots, peeled and sliced

2 medium onions, quartered

2 garlic cloves

2 bay leaves

A small bunch of parsley

2 tablespoons apple cider vinegar

1 teaspoon whole black peppercorns

A small knob of ginger, peeled (optional)

Preheat the oven to 350°F. Lay the bones on an oven pan, and roast for about 30 minutes, or until just browning.

Transfer them to a large stockpot, and cover with water. Place the pot over high heat, and slowly bring to a boil. Watch the pot very carefully as it comes to a boil, scooping off the scum that forms on the surface. Once the water is about to boil, and no more scum is forming, add the rest of the ingredients (no salt!), and bring back to a boil, then quickly transfer to the smallest ring. Reduce the heat to its lowest setting, and simmer very gently, keeping the pot covered with a tight-fitting lid. The longer you cook the broth, the more nutritional benefits you gain: I cook mine for a minimum of 6 hours and up to 24 hours sometimes, adding a little water as needed. If you're cooking this for a long time, it's best to do it in the oven—that way it won't dry out. Simply transfer everything to an ovenproof pot with a lid and put in the oven at 225°F and cook for as long as you need.

Remove the bones, and allow the broth to cool before transferring it to the fridge or freezer. When you are ready to use the broth, either strain it through a fine-mesh strainer, or reheat, and drink it with the lovely veggies that have been cooked with it. Enjoy.

Vegetable broth/stock.

Vegetable stock is really very easy to make and tastes delicious. It's wonderful as a hot drink, but also as a base for risotto, soups, stews, casseroles, pies, and so much more. You could use this stock in place of chicken stocks in other recipes. My recipe is deliberately quite neutral in flavor, which makes it incredibly versatile, but feel free to add any of the suggested optional extras for additional flavor.

---

3 onions, unpeeled, washed and quartered

6 carrots, washed and roughly chopped (peel if not organic)

4 celery stalks, washed and chopped or sliced (leaves too, if liked)

6 thyme sprigs

4 bay leaves

A large handful of parsley, stalks included

1 teaspoon whole black peppercorns

2 garlic cloves, lightly bashed

Filtered or spring water (enough to cover)

OPTIONAL EXTRAS

Leftover organic vedge peelings from the kitchen

Leeks

Fennel

Lemons

Tomatoes

Mushrooms, including the stems (can be dried mushrooms)

Parsnips

Dried or fresh herbs, such as oregano, rosemary, dill, and marjoram

Place the onions on a flat baking sheet under a hot broiler and scorch until the flesh and the skins catch a little—you want a light bit of burn on the edges. Remove, then add to a large stockpot. (You can also do this in a hot pan with a little ghee.) Lightly burning the onions adds an immense amount of flavor to the finished vegetable stock.

Add the other vegetables, herbs, and peppercorns (no salt!) to the pot, cover with water, and place over high heat. When it comes to a boil, skim off any scum that rises to the surface. Reduce the heat to a bare simmer, cover the pot with a tight-fitting lid, and simmer for 1 hour. Remove all the vegetables and herbs with a pair of tongs, then pour the stock through a fine mesh strainer into a bowl.

Decant the stock into glass jars, and transfer to the fridge when cool. The stock will keep for several days in the fridge.

Breakfast broth with poached eggs, kale, and sauerkraut.

ENOUGH FOR 2-3

This is one of the most nourishing, restorative breakfasts you could possibly have, which also happens to be absolutely satisfying and delicious. Many cultures have savory breakfasts as a staple and it's a great habit to get into as a way of cutting down on the sugary start to the day that has become all too common.

---

1 quart homemade chicken broth (or lamb/ beef or fish)

2 handfuls of kale, stalks removed and chopped (or other leafy green of your choice)

2 or 3 eggs (or 6, if you would like 2 each)

1 teaspoon virgin raw coconut oil (optional but very good for digestion and skin)

2 tablespoons roughly chopped parsley or cilantro

4 tablespoons sauerkraut, see pages 145–147 (my favorite is the spicy red cabbage sauerkraut)

Sea salt and freshly ground black pepper

Bring the broth to a gentle boil in a medium but wide saucepan. Add the kale, then gently lower in the eggs to poach in the simmering broth. Remove from the heat when the whites have cooked, but the yolks are still very soft.

Season with sea salt and black pepper, and spoon into waiting bowls. Add the coconut oil, if using, ½ teaspoon or a little more per bowl, sprinkle over the parsley, and then spoon in the sauerkraut and a little of the juice, too.

Drink, eat, slurp, and enjoy an amazing start to the day.

Anti-inflammatory coconut, ginger, and turmeric soup.

SERVES 3-4

This heavenly bowl of goodness really is a delicious way to nourish yourself when you are under the weather, or just feeling depleted, exhausted, and over-tired. Any recipe prepared with broth provides nourishment, but the ingredients in this soup give added benefit if you are feeling poorly or need some TLC. This is a perfect bowl of warming goodness for those rainy and cold wintry days when sustenance of the highest order is completely necessary. I like to have extra bone broth frozen in batches in the freezer, so when I need to make up a batch of this life-saver, it's super-easy, and only takes minutes to make.

---

1 quart homemade chicken broth (see page 136) or my vedge broth (see left)

1¾ cups full-fat coconut milk

A knob of fresh ginger, peeled and very finely sliced

½ teaspoon ground turmeric or a knob of fresh turmeric, finely sliced

Juice of ½–1 lemon (add desired amount)

¼ teaspoon red chili flakes or cayenne pepper

A small handful of cilantro, roughly chopped

2 teaspoons raw virgin coconut oil

Sea salt and freshly ground black pepper

Put all the ingredients, except for the cilantro and coconut oil, into a medium saucepan, and bring to a gentle simmer. Simmer for 5–10 minutes, remove from the heat, and allow to cool for a few minutes. Season with sea salt, and plenty of black pepper, sprinkle over the cilantro, and spoon in the coconut oil. Taste and add more lemon juice if you like, and serve.

Tip: Do be generous with the black pepper as it's been proved that the piperine contained in pepper helps the main potent active ingredient (curcumin) in turmeric to be fully absorbed by the body during digestion. Turmeric is a powerful antioxidant and anti-inflammatory, and has been proved highly effective in reducing the risk of many chronic diseases.

A classic fish stock.

MAKES ABOUT 2 QUARTS

This stock is a great base for fish soups and stews, or smoked fish pies. You can also drink it as a broth. Fish broth is the most nourishing of all broths, containing many trace minerals that support immune function. Just be sure only to use white fish; oily fish are no good for making broth, as the delicate fish oils can become rancid during the cooking process.

---

2 tablespoons butter or ghee

2 onions, quartered

1 carrot, peeled and coarsely chopped

½ cup dry white wine or vermouth

1 large whole fish frame (or 2 small ones), including the head (snapper, bass, sole, turbot work well; no oily fish), gills removed

Filtered or spring water (about 2 quarts, enough to cover the fish frame)

A small bunch of fresh thyme

A small bunch of parsley, stalks included

2 bay leaves

Place a large pot over medium heat, and add the butter. When it is melting, add the onions and carrot, reduce the heat to low, and cook for 20 minutes, stirring occasionally. When the vegetables are lovely and soft, add the wine, increase the heat to medium, and bring just to a boil. Add the fish frames and heads, and enough water to cover the bones.

Bring to a bare simmer, and carefully skim off any scum that rises to the surface. Add the herbs, and keep the heat low. Cook at a bare simmer for 1 hour, occasionally skimming off any scum. Add a little more water if needed to keep the bones covered.

When the stock is done, remove the solids with a pair of tongs, then strain the lot through a fine-mesh strainer. At this point you can use the stock in other dishes that require fish stock, or you can pour the stock into glass jars and allow to cool before transferring to the fridge or freezer. It will keep in the fridge for about five days, or in the freezer for many months.

A warming golden fish broth.

MAKES ABOUT 1½–2 QUARTS

This is my favorite way to drink fish broth. I like the freshness it has, as opposed to the classic fish stock, which I find is better as a base for fish soups and stews. I enjoy drinking a cup of this before my evening meal. It also happens to be incredibly anti-inflammatory, which is a wonderful thing for anyone suffering from any kind of inflammatory disease. Not only is this soup a form of medicine, but it tastes wonderful too.

---

1 large whole fish frame (or 2 small ones), including the head (snapper, bass, sole and turbot work well; no oily fish), gills removed

Filtered or spring water (about 2 quarts, enough to cover the fish frame)

2 onions, quartered

1 carrot, peeled and coarsely chopped

A knob of ginger, peeled and sliced

A small knob of fresh turmeric root

1 teaspoon black peppercorns

A bunch of cilantro, leaves and stalks

1 lemongrass stalk, bashed

2 kaffir lime leaves

Sea salt

Place a large pot over medium heat, add the fish frames and heads, and enough water to cover the bones. Bring to a bare simmer, and carefully skim off any scum that rises to the surface.

Add the onions, carrot, ginger, turmeric, and black peppercorns, and bring back to a boil. Add the cilantro, lemongrass, and kaffir lime leaves, then reduce the heat once more to low. Cook at a bare simmer for 1 hour, occasionally skimming off the scum if any rises to the top. Add more water if needed, to keep the bones covered.

When the stock is done, remove the solids with a pair of tongs, then strain the lot through a fine-mesh strainer. Either serve as it is, seasoned with just enough salt, or pour the broth into glass jars, and allow to cool before transferring to the fridge or freezer. It will keep in the fridge for about five days, or in the freezer for many months.

A few words and tips on Lacto-fermentation.

What is lacto-fermentation? Why is it good for you?

Lacto-fermentation is a method of preserving food that transforms fresh food into favorites such as pickles, chutney, miso, tempeh, kimchi, and sauerkraut. Fermentation is as old as life itself; humans have been fermenting fruit and vegetables for millennia. It was a safe and delicious way of preserving foods and drinks before refrigeration.

Most people think about beer or wine when they hear the term fermentation. Yeasts are used to convert the sugars in grains or grape juice into alcohol, whereas bacteria are responsible for lacto-fermentation. The "lacto" part of the term refers to a specific species of bacteria, namely lactobacillus. Various strains of these bacteria are present on the surface of all plants, especially those growing close to the ground, and are also plentiful within the entire gastrointestinal tract, including the mouths and genitals of humans, and other animal species.

The lactobacillus strain is so named because it was first studied in milk ferments. However, lacto-fermentation does not necessarily involve dairy products. The Lactobacillus bacteria convert lactose or other sugars into lactic acid, which is a natural preservative that inhibits the growth of harmful bacteria. Apart from preservation advantages, lacto-fermentation also increases or maintains the vitamin and enzyme levels of the fermented food, and improves its digestibility.

The traditional diets of every society have included some kind of lacto-fermented food. Europeans consume lacto-fermented dairy products, sauerkraut, grape leaves, herbs, and root vegetables. The Alaskan Inuit ferment fish and sea mammals. The Orient is known for pickled vegetables, sauces, and kimchi in particular. Farming societies in central Africa are known for porridges made from soured grains. Pickles and relishes are part of the American food tradition. Since the advent of industrialization, most commercial pickling is done with vinegar and sugar, which offer more predictable results, but no lactic acid or probiotics. With just a little patience, instruction, and minimal supplies, it is possible to learn the time-honored art of lacto-fermentation. They are easy for even a beginner to prepare, and it doesn't take long to gain enough confidence to venture beyond basic yogurt or sauerkraut to an endless variety of fruits, vegetables, beverages, and more.

One of the benefits of eating fermented foods, aside from their delicious flavor, is the huge health benefit. They are so packed with enzymes and multiple strains of good bacteria, that eating a portion daily can significantly help to heal the gut, increase immunity, balance hormones, improve bowel health, aid digestion, and much more. They are cheap to make, and require fewer ingredients and equipment than the more modern method of pickling using vinegar and sugar. Win-win, I'd say.

The important thing is not to be intimidated by lacto-fermentation. Unless it smells unmistakably putrid (in which case common sense says throw it away), fermented foods are some of the safest foods we can eat.

Be sure to use a good-quality sea salt with no anti-caking agents.

Use fresh spring water or filtered tap water that is fluoride- and chlorine-free. The chemicals will kill the good bacteria and cause the fermenting vegetables to rot instead of ferment. If chlorinated tap water doesn't allow friendly bacteria to grow, and actually causes the fermenting vegetables to putrefy, imagine what it does to your gut when you drink it... worth thinking about!

If you don't have a special weight to hold down the vegetables as many recipes suggest, you can improvise and use a cabbage leaf, folded into the right shape, and tucked into the top of the jar, to keep the vegetables submerged under the pickling brine.

A magical golden kraut.

Garlic, ginger, and turmeric are a magical combination used in many health tonics. Turmeric has been used in Ayurvedic medicine and Indian cooking for thousands of years. This amazing spice contains bioactive compounds with powerful medicinal properties—it is antiviral, antifungal, antibacterial, and anti-inflammatory. Turmeric drastically increases the body's antioxidant capacity, because the main active ingredient in turmeric, curcumin, happens to be a potent antioxidant. Curcumin supports brain and heart health, and heals the gut. Including turmeric regularly in your diet results in changes on a molecular level that may help prevent, and perhaps even treat cancer. Ginger is also a powerful anti-inflammatory, it aids digestion, and can help with nausea. Garlic is a natural antibiotic, and also contains prebiotics, which help support the growth of good bacteria within the gut. So not only is this golden kraut super-tasty, it's a jarful of wonderful healing stuff.

For an extra dose of goodness, cover this kraut with extra brine, so that you can drink it all on its own for a shot of probiotics, enzymes, and all the wonderful properties of the spices involved. You can also add it to broth (see page 141 for ideas).

---

4 pounds white cabbage, finely shredded

18 ounces carrots, grated

1 garlic bulb, minced

4 tablespoons grated ginger

2 tablespoons freshly grated turmeric

2 teaspoons caraway seeds

2 teaspoon fennel seeds

1 teaspoon finely ground black pepper

3–5 tablespoons pure sea salt

EQUIPMENT

2 or 3 large glass jars (about 1 quart each) or 5 or 6 smaller ones, sterilized (see page 79)

Put the cabbage in a large bowl along with all the other ingredients, initially with only 3 tablespoons of sea salt. Pound the cabbage for a few minutes using a cabbage pounder, or if you don't have one, throw on a pair of latex gloves, and massage the cabbage by hand—just keep going until the cabbage is breaking down, and releasing all its lovely juices. Taste for salt, and adjust as needed. The kraut should not be too salty, but should have plenty of flavor brought out by the salt. Keep pounding or massaging with your hands until the cabbage breaks down further, and releases all its juices. This process can take a little while, at least 15 minutes, because you need enough liquid to cover the cabbage in its own brine when pressed down in the jars.

Put the cabbage mix into one or two glass jars, pressing the cabbage down hard to submerge it in the brine. If necessary, add some lightly salted water to cover the vegetables. Cover with a tight-fitting lid, and set aside on the worktop away from any heat source, and leave it to ferment. You must "burp" the cabbage once a day to release the pressure, or your jar may explode. To do this, slowly open the lid and allow the gases to escape, before carefully replacing the lid.

Leave the sauerkraut to culture at room temperature (59–68°F is preferred) until the desired flavor is reached. I find five days is about right, but it can take anything from three to seven, or eight days, depending on the temperature in your kitchen. I like to start tasting my batch after about three days, and finish the ferment when I like the flavor. If I want a stronger ferment, I tend to leave it the full eight days, but tasting gives you a good indication of where it's at. Alternatively, if it is fermenting in a very cool place—say, a cool, dark cellar—then you can leave it for several weeks, if not months. The longer and slower the fermentation process, the more flavor it develops.

Once the kraut is finished, transfer it to a very cool place, preferably the fridge, and allow it to mature for one month. Once opened, consume within a few weeks.

Spicy red cabbage sauerkraut.

MAKES 3 PINT JARS

This is my take on a naturally fermented pickle I came across from a fantastic online shop based in the UK called The Cultured Cellar. I came up with this recipe because I travel a lot, and wanted to enjoy it in other countries. Made with red cabbage and beets, it's a bit spicy, a bit tangy, and deeply delicious. Try it with cold meats, in a sandwich, with roast meat and salad, or with cheese and crackers.

1 medium head of red cabbage, finely shredded	2 teaspoons caraway seeds
1–3 tablespoons sea salt	1 red chile, seeded and finely chopped
1 beet, peeled and cut into tiny cubes	3 garlic cloves, crushed
1 carrot, peeled and grated	EQUIPMENT
1 red onion, finely diced	Cabbage pounder
	3 pint jars, sterilized (see page 79)

Put the cabbage in a large bowl and sprinkle over the salt, starting with 1 tablespoon and adding more to taste as you go. The salt not only helps to break down the cabbage, it also keeps the bad bacteria at bay, so don't be afraid of adding a generous amount. Pound the cabbage with a cabbage pounder or potato masher (or knead with clean hands) for about 10 minutes, or until there is enough liquid to cover the cabbage.

Add the remaining ingredients, and pound or knead again until everything comes together, and is thoroughly mixed.

Stuff the mix into the glass jars, and seal with a tight-fitting lid. Culture at room temperature (59–68°F is preferred) until the desired flavor is achieved (start tasting after three days). I usually leave mine for about five days, and then transfer to the fridge, but it can take as little as three, or as long as seven to eight days.

Once you have transferred the sauerkraut to the fridge, leave it for an additional three to four weeks for the flavors to develop before eating.

Mexican pickled red onions.

MAKES 1 HALF-PINT JAR
(A LITTLE GOES A LONG WAY)

These pretty pink pickles are a typical topping for Yucatan-style pork or seafood dishes. I love serving them with my cauliflower or quinoa tortillas, salsa, and some slow-cooked pork, or pan-fried fish to make delicious Mexican tortillas. You could also add some refried beans for serious indulgence. Onions contain high amounts of prebiotics. These are non-digestible fibers that make their way through the digestive tract, and they are what the probiotics feed on, so by eating lots of prebiotics, you are supporting the growth of all the friendly bacteria within your gut. Win-win again.

20 whole black peppercorns	1 large red onion, thinly sliced into half moons
8 allspice berries	¾ teaspoon fine sea salt
1 whole clove	¼ cup raw apple cider vinegar
½ generous teaspoon Mexican dried oregano	¼ cup freshly squeezed lime juice

Start by pounding the peppercorns, allspice berries, clove, and oregano, using a mortar and pestle until you have a rough powder.

Put the onion into a medium bowl with the spice mixture and salt. Use your hands to firmly scrunch and massage the onion, tossing lightly as you do. Add the vinegar and lime juice, and toss well.

Transfer the mixture to a clean glass jar with a tight-fitting lid, and put in the fridge to marinate for 24 hours. Give the jar an occasional shake.

The pickled onions will keep in the fridge for up to five days.

Fermented vegetables.

MAKES 1 1-QUART JAR

These are the perfect ferment for the beginner, as you really can't go wrong. They are super-tasty; even the kids love them. I often put a small plate on the dinner table just before I serve the evening meal, as the pickles help us digest food due to the high amount of enzymes and probiotics. They are also immune-boosting and gut- healing. They will last for months in the fridge, and will actually get more flavorsome as time goes by. My two favorite combinations are carrots with cauliflower and radishes with dill, both super-easy and wonderfully delicious.

Never use chlorinated faucet water when fermenting. The chlorine will stop the good bacteria from flourishing, and the veggies will simply rot.

Start by making the salt brine: dissolve the salt in the cold water and set aside.

Place your chosen veggies into the glass jar, tip in the spices and leaves, and pour over the brine. Cover the jar with a tight-fitting lid, and place on a worktop or pantry shelf to ferment. Culture at room temperature (59-68°F is preferred) until the desired flavor and texture are achieved. This can take anywhere from three days, and up to seven, depending on how warm your kitchen is. You will need to burp the pickles daily to release excess pressure. To do this, slowly open the lid and allow the gases to escape, before carefully placing the lid back on. This will prevent your jar from exploding under the pressure that fermenting causes.

Once the vegetables are finished, transfer the jar to the fridge or a cold cellar. The flavors will continue to develop with time.

The pickles are ready to eat once chilled, and will last for many months in the fridge. Don't throw away the pickle juice: it's amazing added to bowls of broth for a little flavor and probiotic boost, and can also be used as a starter to speed up the process for the next jar of pickles. You could also add a little to salad dressings.

EQUIPMENT
1-quart jar, sterilized (see page 79)
2 tablespoons sea salt
1 quart filtered or spring water (must be chlorine-free)
Enough raw veggies to tightly fill a 1-quart glass jar

For the carrots and cauliflower
3 garlic cloves, very slightly crushed, but still intact
⅔ (roughly) whole cauliflower cut into florets, rinsed in cold water (or enough to fill your jar)
3–4 large carrots, cut into chunky bite-size pieces
2 teaspoons of Za'atar (see page 108), or 2–3 teaspoons whole coriander seeds
3 fresh bay leaves
2 teaspoons whole black peppercorns

For the radishes with dill
Enough small radishes to fill your jar, halved
4 sprigs of fresh dill
½ teaspoon dill seeds
½ teaspoon brown mustard seeds
1 teaspoon caraway seeds
1 teaspoon black peppercorns
1 bay leaf

Wild fermented spicy dill
and cucumber pickles.

MAKES 1 2½-QUART JAR

These beautifully crunchy and tasty pickles are a great way of using up a glut of cucumbers. They are great as an accompaniment for cheese or for making tartare sauce if you use the smaller sized cucumbers. As they are naturally fermented, they are jam-packed with gut-friendly probiotics, which boost the immune system, support a healthy digestive system and promote the growth of friendly bacteria within the micro biome (gut).

EQUIPMENT

2 quart jars plus 1 pint jar or 1 2½-quart jar, sterilized (see page 79)

5 tablespoons sea salt

2½ quarts chlorine-free water—filtered or spring water is best

3 teaspoons black peppercorns

1½ teaspoons red pepper flakes

1 tablespoon yellow mustard seeds

2 teaspoons coriander seeds

6–10 garlic cloves

2 bunches of dill

Pickling cucumbers, medium or small, to fill your jars

Tannin-containing leaf (see right)

Dissolve the sea salt in the cold water. Set aside. Mix the spices together in a small bowl and set aside.

Place the cloves, a few of the sprigs of dill, and half the spices in a large glass or ceramic mixing bowl. Mix lightly to combine, and place this mixture in the jar/s.

Pack half the cucumbers tightly on top of the spices. Repeat with a layer of garlic and spices, add another tightly packed layer of cucumbers, and top them off with more garlic and spices.

Pour the brine over the pickles, leaving a little bit of headspace at the top of the jar to allow for the ferment to expand. Place a tannin-containing leaf (see right) on top of the pickles as a cover between the pickles and the surface of the brine. You can use a cabbage leaf instead, to keep the pickles under the brine.

Cover the jar with a tight-fitting lid and ferment at a steady room temperature (59–68°F is preferred) until you like they way they taste. This can take anywhere from three or four days up to a full week, depending on how warm your kitchen is. These pickles will stay crunchy, and will taste better if they can ferment in quite a cool place, but not as cold as the fridge. Burp daily to release excess pressure—if too much pressure builds up, the jars can explode.

As the cucumbers ferment, the brine may turn cloudy, and the pickling liquor will become fizzy and tangy. The pickles should taste deliciously tangy and sourish when done. Eat immediately, or store in the refrigerator for several months, eating as and when you like.

Keeping cucumbers crunchy during fermentation

Add a tannin-containing agent to the pickling jars. Black tea leaves, oak leaves, grape leaves, or horseradish leaves all work well. Add a few larger leaves or a good teaspoon or so of loose tea or a teabag to a 2-quart jar.

Ferment at the coolest temperature you can achieve. A fast, hot fermentation can result in a less-than-stellar crunch to a pickle.

Try small, whole cucumbers first. They tend to retain their crunch better than a chopped-up larger cucumber.

Remove the blossom end—it contains enzymes that soften pickles. Removing it will preserve the firm texture.

If the cucumber is harvested a bit later in the year, or has been on the vine a little longer, it will develop a thicker skin. Use a skewer or paring knife to prick a hole in each cucumber. The brine can penetrate faster, and the cucumbers will culture more evenly.

Pickled lemons.

MAKES 1 1½-QUART JAR

These deliciously tangy pickled lemons work really well in yogurt sauces or dressings. The flavor of the lemons works really well in Moroccan dishes, especially tagines, or slow, meltingly tender roasts. Because they are naturally fermented, they will give you a massive boost of vitamin C, as well as loads of beneficial friendly bacteria. They keep for up to two years in the pantry.

EQUIPMENT
1½-quart glass jar or fermenting crock, sterilized (see page 79)

10–12 unwaxed lemons, depending on size (thin-skinned lemons work very well), sliced into thin rings then into half moons
4 tablespoons plain kombucha or raw apple cider vinegar

1 cup lemon juice
6 tablespoons sea salt
1 bay leaf
1 cinnamon stick
½ teaspoon cloves
½ teaspoon coriander seeds
½ teaspoon black peppercorns
Filtered water, at room temperature

Put the lemon slices into the clean jar or crock, and compress slightly with the back of your hand. Mix the kombucha or vinegar with the lemon juice in a bowl, and add the salt.

Pour the lemon juice mixture into the jar. Sprinkle over the seasonings, pushing the bay leaf down the side of the jar, along with the cinnamon stick. Use the handle of a wooden spoon to release any air bubbles. Top the mixture off with filtered water to 1 inch below the rim of the jar. Give the jar a little swirl to mix the water with the brine.

Cover the jar with a tight-fitting lid, and set aside on the worktop or pantry shelf. Culture at room temperature (59–68°F is preferred) for two to three weeks. Burp the lemons daily—slowly open the lid, and let the ferment breathe for a minute before putting the lid back on.

Once the lemons are finished, store somewhere cold, or in the fridge. The flavors will continue to develop, even in the fridge.

To use your lemons, scoop the pulp away and use the skin, thinly sliced, or use both the pulp and skin according to your taste.

Kimchi.

MAKES 1 1-QUART JAR

If you have never had this amazing pickle before, you may be a little wary, going by its smell, but if you love bold flavors, chile, and pickles, then this is going to hit the spot. Try to find Korean red pepper flakes, which have a slightly sweet smoky flavor. Otherwise, use any red pepper flakes, but the flavor will not be quite like the original. I am totally addicted to its wonderfully sour taste—like pickles, but without the vinegar. Because it's naturally fermented, like sauerkraut, it's incredibly good for your immune system and digestion.

EQUIPMENT

Latex gloves (optional)
1-quart glass jar, sterilized (see page 79) with a tight-fitting lid

1 large Chinese cabbage
6⅓ tablespoons sea salt
Several quarts of spring water or mineral water (or filtered water, as long as it's chlorine free)
1 tablespoon grated garlic (about 5–6 medium cloves)
1 teaspoon grated ginger
1 teaspoon unrefined sugar
4 tablespoons good-quality fish sauce
1–5 tablespoons Korean red pepper flakes (or use any red pepper flakes if you can't find the Korean)
1 daikon, peeled and cut into matchsticks
4 scallions, trimmed, and cut into 2-inch pieces

Quarter the cabbage lengthwise, and remove the inner cores. Cut each quarter across into 1¼-inch strips.

Tip the cabbage into a large bowl, and using your hands, gently massage the salt into the cabbage until it starts to soften a little— this will take 1–2 minutes. Once it has softened, add enough water to cover the cabbage. Place a plate over the top, and weigh it down with an unopened jar or can. Set it aside and let it sit for 1–2 hours.

Pour off the brine into a separate bowl or pitcher and reserve.

Rinse the cabbage under cold running water, then let it sit in a colander for about 10 minutes to drain—you may need to pat it dry with a clean dishtowel to remove any excess water. Set aside.

To make the paste, combine the garlic, ginger, sugar, and fish sauce in a small bowl, and mix to form a paste. Mix in the Korean red pepper flakes, using 1 tablespoon for mild or up to 5 tablespoons (which is what I like) for a more fiery taste.

Take the large bowl used for salting the cabbage, make sure it is clean, then put in all the vegetables and the paste, again using your hands to bring it all together, massaging the seasoning into the veggies really well. You can use Latex gloves for this to protect your hands from chile, or stains, or smells.

Pack the kimchi into the clean jar, pressing it down really well. Pour in enough of the reserved brine to cover all the veggies completely—you won't need much, but everything needs to be submerged. Leave about 1½ inches of headspace at the top of the jar.

Seal the jar, and leave at room temperature for between three and five days, longer if you're feeling brave. I like to leave mine for five days. You will see bubbles inside the jar and brine may seep out the top, so sit the jar in a bowl, or on a plate to catch the overflow.

Check the kimchi once a day, pressing down the veggies with a clean spoon to keep them submerged—this will release the gases created during the fermentation process. You can taste it each day, starting from around day three, to check for desired sourness and ripeness.

When it's ready, place the kimchi in the fridge. You can eat it immediately, but it's best if you leave it for a couple of weeks to develop. Kimchi is now a staple in my household, I am completely addicted.

Blackberry and elderberry vinegar.

MAKES 3⅓ CUPS

Homemade vinegars are a wonderful ingredient to have in your kitchen. Good-quality vinegar is a must when making delicious salad dressings, and making your own vinegar will yield amazing results. You can make your own mother vinegar, but I have chosen just to add the flavored kinds here, which are really easy to make.

This vinegar is best used in dressings for salads that contain autumn's finest offerings, such as pears, apples, and walnuts. It would also go beautifully sprinkled over roast beets, and slow-cooked roast meats for an added dimension of fruity flavor. It works beautifully in place of balsamic vinegar in salads, and goes particularly well with goat cheese.

Don't be alarmed by the amount of sugar in the recipe: as the fruit ferments, the sugars are eaten up by the time the vinegar is ready.

EQUIPMENT
1-quart glass jar with a rubber seal, sterilized (see page 79)

2½ cups raw apple cider vinegar
½ cup unrefined golden granulated sugar
14 ounces blackberries
4 ounces elderberries (or use extra blackberries, or any other seasonal berries)

Combine the vinegar and sugar in a medium saucepan, and stir gently over moderately low heat. Stir until the sugar is dissolved, then remove from the heat, and set aside to cool completely.

Put the berries into the clean jar, and crush them gently with a wooden spoon or fork. Pour in the cold sweetened vinegar, and seal with the lid.

Set aside in a cool, dark place to ferment. This process can take about one to two weeks, after which time the vinegar should smell sweet and fruity. Strain the vinegar, discarding the pulp. Pour the liquid into a clean glass jar or bottle.

The vinegar will keep for a good eight to nine months.

Variation: Raspberry vinegar

I love to use this vinegar to dress salads that contain summer fruit, such as grilled peaches and soft berries. Combine it with olive oil and black pepper as a dressing for baby spinach and peppery salad leaves. Use to deglaze cooking pans after sautéing lamb or liver. It adds a fruity depth to the caramelized flavors in the pan. Crazy as it sounds, it is also seriously delicious drizzled over vanilla ice cream. For another twist, try it in a refreshing drink: pour over ice, then top up with mineral water or lemonade.

Use 18 ounces raspberries in place of the blackberries and elderberries and follow the recipe above.

You can also make herb or flower vinegars by placing herbs/flowers in white wine vinegar or apple cider vinegar, and leaving them to steep for a few days or weeks to impart their flavor. Herbs and flowers that work particularly well are:
Chive flowers
Tarragon
Elderflowers
Rose petals

Spiced almond crackers.

MAKES 20

Grain and gluten-free

These crackers are a cinch to make, are light and crispy, and go well with many different toppings. A personal favorite is my chicken liver pâté (see page 102) with dill pickles on the side (see page 149), but try these with cheeses, chutneys, and all sorts of dips.

2 cups ground almonds
1 extra-large egg
½ teaspoon sea salt flakes, plus a little extra
½ teaspoon freshly ground black pepper, plus a little extra

1 tablespoon finely chopped rosemary
½ teaspoon thyme leaves
1 teaspoon fennel seeds

Preheat the oven to 325°F, and line a baking sheet with waxed paper.

Put the ground almonds in a food processor with the egg, salt, and pepper. Pulse until a dough forms. Turn out the dough, and place between two sheets of nonstick parchment paper or waxed paper—no need to flour or dust the dough, as the oils in the nuts should prevent it from sticking.

Roll out the dough to roughly ⅛ inch thick. Carefully peel off the top layer of paper, then sprinkle with salt and pepper, and then the rosemary, thyme, and fennel seeds. Cut into squares, 2–2¾ inches, using a very sharp knife.

Using a palette knife or butter knife, transfer the crackers to the prepared sheet, and bake in the middle (not the top) of the oven for 12–14 minutes, but check them after 6–8 minutes. Because these crackers are made with nuts, not flour, they burn very easily, so they may be ready in less than the recommended cooking time.

When they are nicely golden, remove them from the oven and set aside to cool before transferring to an airtight tin or jar. These crackers are best eaten within a couple of days.

A spiced almond and coconut bread.

MAKES 2 LOAVES

Grain and gluten-free · Paleo

This bread couldn't be easier to make, and is heavenly spread thickly with salty butter and honey, or topped with any number of savory toppings. It makes great toast, and it also freezes well. These lovely loaves are packed full of protein, essential fatty acids, and fiber, and are very nourishing, as well as delicious.

EQUIPMENT
2 1-pound nonstick loaf pans

3 cups ground almonds
4 tablespoons coconut flour
generous ½ cup golden flaxseed meal
½ teaspoon sea salt
2½ teaspoons baking soda
10 eggs

½ cup coconut oil or olive oil
2 tablespoons honey
2 tablespoons apple cider vinegar
2 teaspoons caraway seeds
2 teaspoons fennel seeds
2 teaspoons fresh or dried chopped rosemary
sea salt and freshly ground black pepper

Preheat the oven to 325°F, and grease or line the loaf pans.

Put the almonds, flour, flaxseed, salt, baking soda, eggs, oil, honey, and vinegar into a large food processor or mixer, and whizz or beat until thoroughly combined. This may take a few minutes, and you might need to stop and scrape down the sides of the bowl before mixing again. When it's completely mixed, pour the batter into the prepared pans. It will be quite a wet batter, but that's ok.

Sprinkle over the seeds, rosemary, and some sea salt, and a generous pinch of black pepper.

Bake for about 40 minutes. Cool for 10 minutes before turning the loaves out of their pans, and serve fresh or toasted. This bread lasts well for a few days in or out of the fridge.

Perfectly cooked quinoa.

SERVES 2-3

Quinoa can be soggy and soapy-tasting, but here are a few simple tips to guarantee it turns out fluffy and nutritious without a hint of soap. Soaking is key, and cooking it in bone broth (optional) can ramp up the nutrition stakes massively, while simultaneously making it more flavorsome and easily digested. Quinoa has enzyme inhibitors (otherwise known as phytates) in its coating, and these can make the cooked quinoa taste soapy. They also make quinoa less digestible, and eating it requires many of your body's own store of enzymes and minerals to be used in the digestion process, contributing to loss of bone density, and tooth decay. This is not a problem if your diet is low in phytates, but if you eat nuts, pulses, grains, and the like on a regular basis, it's a good idea always to soak them first for better digestion, maximum nutrition, and strong bones and teeth well into old age.

Scant 1 cup quinoa
3¼ cups filtered water
1 teaspoon apple cider vinegar
2 cups chicken bone broth (see page 136) or water

Sea salt
A knob of butter (optional, but delicious, and will ensure you absorb all the fat-soluble vitamins)

Soak the quinoa in the water and vinegar overnight or for at least a few hours. Drain and rinse several times under cold running water.

Put the quinoa, bone broth, and a pinch of salt in a large pot over high heat. Bring to a boil, then lower the heat to a simmer. Cover and cook for about 15 minutes until all the liquid is absorbed (but the quinoa is still wet), and the germs have begun to spiral.

Turn off the heat, place a sheet of paper towels between the pot and the lid, and leave to sit for at least 5 minutes. Fluff up with a fork before serving. Serve the quinoa as a base for a hearty meat or vegetarian topping, or turn into a delicious salad by adding fresh or roast veggies and fresh herbs, a drizzle of olive oil, salt and pepper, and a good squeeze of lemon juice.

Perfectly cooked puy lentils.

SERVES 2-3

Grain and gluten-free

Puy lentils are a wonderful addition to salads, lending deep and earthy tones. They are a great alternative to grains as a base for a meal, too. They last well in the fridge, so whipping up midweek meals is easy and nutritious—all they need is some roasted squash, hummus, and arugula leaves, a drizzle of olive oil, and a squeeze of lemon, and you have a heavenly quick lunch or supper in minutes.

I love cooking lentils in bone broth. I finds it softens their flavor, but you can cook them in water or vedge stock if you wish. You don't need to soak them for cooking purposes, but I like to soak them overnight to reduce the phytates.

---

1 cup puy lentils (give them a good rinse if you don't have time to soak them)
1 teaspoon apple cider vinegar or baking soda

2½ cups chicken bone broth (see page 136), water, or vedge stock (see page 140)

Soak the lentils overnight in enough water to keep them submerged, along with the vinegar or baking soda. Drain, and rinse several times under cold running water.

Put the lentils in a saucepan, and pour over the bone broth. Turn the heat up, and bring to a gentle simmer. Reduce the heat to a bare simmer, and cook for 20–25 minutes, or until the lentils are tender, but still have a slight bite to them. Drain and serve.

Cauliflower tortillas.

MAKES 6-8

Grain and gluten-free

These are super-easy to make—my perfect go-to tortilla recipe for when I feel like a Mexican feast. Cauliflower is truly versatile, it's low carb and full of fiber, and with the protein from the eggs, these pale beauties are wonderfully nutritious.

EQUIPMENT
Steamer
Cheesecloth

1 medium–large head of cauliflower, cut into chunks
Juice of ½ lime

1 teaspoon finely chopped oregano
½ teaspoon smoked paprika
2 extra-large eggs, beaten
Sea salt and freshly ground or cracked black pepper

Preheat the oven to 350°F. Put a cheesecloth over a large bowl, and line a baking sheet with baking parchment. Set up a pan with a steamer over the top, big enough to hold the riced cauliflower. Put a few inches of water in the pan, and place over high heat. Bring the water to a boil.

Meanwhile, put the cauliflower into a food processor, and pulse until finer than rice grains. Pop into the steamer over the boiling water for about 5 minutes, covered.

Tip the steamed cauliflower into the bowl lined with cheesecloth, and let cool for a few minutes, then pull up the sides of the cloth and squeeze—as strong as you can; you need to get most of the liquid out, or your tortillas will be soggy! Transfer to a clean bowl, discarding the liquid.

Add the lime juice, oregano, paprika, and seasoning to the dry cauliflower, tip in the eggs, and mix everything really well to thoroughly combine. Shape the mixture into 6–8 balls of equal size and spread them onto the prepared baking sheet to make equal circles about the size of a small tortilla, not too thick, and not too thin.

Transfer to the oven and bake for 8–10 minutes, then flip them over and bake for an additional 5 minutes. Set aside. When you are ready to eat, toast them in a really hot dry pan to add a slightly charred flavor, which is totally delicious.

Buckwheat tortillas.

MAKES 8-10

Grain and gluten-free

Delicious for making enchiladas and quesadillas, a cinch to prepare—much easier than you might imagine—and the dough freezes well, so you could always make a double batch, and freeze half, so that next time you are set to go with minimum fuss.

2½ cups buckwheat flour (or quinoa flour), plus extra for dusting
Generous pinch of sea salt

¾ cup cold water
1 tablespoon melted virgin coconut oil, plus a little extra

Mix the flour and salt in a large bowl. Add the water and oil and bring together with your fingers until you have a slightly tacky dough. Shape the dough into a ball, flattening it slightly with the heel of your hand. You have the right consistency when the edges don't crack. Add more flour or water as needed.

Turn out the dough onto a floured surface, and divide into 9 equal portions. Roll them into balls, then cover with a damp cloth. Using plenty of extra flour, roll out each ball into a thin circle roughly 6 inches across. You will need to liberally dust both sides to prevent the tortilla from sticking to the work surface, and the utensil you use to slide under it to lift it up.

You need to handle the raw tortillas carefully, because being made with gluten-free flour, they are quite fragile. Once cooked, they become more robust, and will hold together. Stack the rolled tortillas, layered with baking parchment, to prevent sticking.

Heat a heavy cast iron or nonstick skillet over high heat. When the pan is hot, remove the top piece of parchment, and lay the first tortilla into the pan. Cook for 1–2 minutes, or until bubbles start to appear, flip it over, and cook for an additional minute on the other side. Remove from the pan and repeat with the rest.

Stack the cooked tortillas, again layered between baking parchment, and cover with foil or a heavy cloth to keep them warm and supple. Serve immediately.

Sweet Pantry.

This sweet "toolbox" section is a collection of some of my favorite go-to recipes from my wholefood kitchen; quick and easy bakes and treats that can be adapted to suit the seasons. There are also some super-simple sweet spice mixes to add delicious layers of flavor to fruits, granolas, bakes, or puddings. You will also find refined sugar-free jams and syrups, cordials, and dairy-free nut milks that are totally divine, as well as a spiced turmeric milk that makes an amazing gut healing, anti-inflammatory drink for those in need of a little nourishment. There is also my favorite dark rich chocolate and buckwheat brownies, luxuriously soft and sweet fruit butters, cultured yogurts, and other tempting treats.

SWEET PANTRY Sweet Butters and Creams Nut Milks and Custard Jams and Curds Chocolate

Apricot, lavender, and honey butter.

MAKES 2-3 PINT JARS

This beautiful golden-amber colored butter is easy to make, and a great way of using up a glut of apricots. You could also use this heavenly butter to sandwich and decorate cakes, add to your morning fruit and granola, or spread on scones or pancakes. It would also be delightful with thin toast or crackers, and fresh ricotta, or my plain kefir cheese (see page 124).

EQUIPMENT	2⅛ cups fresh apricot juice
Several sterilized glass jars	or nectar
(see page 79)	Heaping ⅓ cup honey
	3-4 tablespoons fresh lemon
3¼ pounds fresh apricots,	juice
halved and pitted	A pinch of salt
	3 sprigs of lavender (optional)

Place all the ingredients, except for the lavender, in a large saucepan, and bring to a gentle boil. Cover, leaving the lid slightly askew, and simmer over medium–high heat, stirring frequently, until the apricots are very tender and yielding. This should take 15–18 minutes.

Uncover the pan and continue to simmer very gently, stirring frequently, until very thick. This will take about 1 hour. Do watch it carefully as you don't want the natural sugars to catch and burn on the bottom of the saucepan. Add a few of the lavender buds, about half a head to start with, and simmer for an additional 5 minutes. Taste and add more lavender if you wish—just be careful not to add too much as the lavender can easily take over if you go too far.

Set aside to cool a little before very carefully spooning the mixture into a food processor, or high-powered blender. Purée until smooth. Transfer the butter to the jars, and let it cool completely. Place the lids on the jars and keep in the fridge. The butter will last for about a week.

Roasted peach and lemon thyme butter.

MAKES 2-3 PINT JARS

The roasting really brings out the deep richness of the peaches and the lemon thyme is a delightful little twist. People often think of woody herbs as being reserved for savory dishes, but I love adding rosemary and thyme to sweet dishes too. Keep a few jars of this heavenly stuff in the fridge, ready to top scones, hot toasted sourdough pancakes or crêpes, cakes or meringues. It is also good served with a little Greek yogurt and granola.

EQUIPMENT	3 pounds peaches
Several sterilized glass jars	Scant ½ cup light honey or
(see page 79)	maple syrup
	Juice of 2 lemons
	5 lemon thyme sprigs, leaves
	only, chopped

You need to remove the skins from the peaches. The easiest way to do this is to immerse the peaches in boiling water for about 30 seconds. Lift them out of the water and, using a paring knife, the skins should slip right off.

Cut the skinned peaches in half, remove and discard the pits, chop up the flesh, then transfer it to a large saucepan along with the honey, lemon juice, and the lemon thyme. Simmer over low heat for about 30 minutes until the fruit starts to fall apart. Blitz the hot bubbling fruit with a stick blender—either leave in some texture, or make it very smooth; I like mine with just a little texture.

Preheat the oven to 350°F. Pour the fruit mixture into a glass baking dish, and bake for about 1 hour, or until it cooks down to a deep golden color. Transfer to the jars, allow to cool, and move to the fridge, where it will keep for a good week.

Gelatin Marshmallows Desserts Baking Sweet Sauces and Sugars Drinks

SWEET PANTRY *Sweet Butters and Creams* Nut Milks and Custard Jams and Curds Chocolate

Salted honey butter.

Honey butter used to be a regular feature in the kitchen cupboard not so long ago, but in recent decades it seems to have all but disappeared. Honey was often added to butter as a way of making it last a little longer, as good old-fashioned raw honey has preserving qualities.

Raw honey is exceptionally good for you, but with butter and a little salt, it becomes something altogether different: creamy, spreadable, sweet, salty, and luscious. You can adjust the flavors by using different kinds of honey, and indeed butter. Try this delectable spread on toast, crêpes, cornbread, muffins, scones, pancakes, cupcakes, waffles, banana bread, and much more.

3½ sticks unsalted butter (raw butter if you can find it)
1 teaspoon sea salt, flaky or fine (if you only have rock salt just grind it to a fine powder)

⅔ cup raw honey (manuka, blossom, or heather honey work well, but any good honey will be delicious)

You can omit the salt, and add salt flakes at the very end instead, so that you get lovely flecks of salt, which add a nice crunch when you eat the butter.

Put all the ingredients in a bowl or food processor, and beat until thoroughly combined. (You can whip the butter to make a lighter consistency if you wish: just mix it in a free-standing cake mixer and beat until light and fluffy.) At this point you can scoop the butter into a jar, or roll it up into a log in some parchment paper and set in the fridge.

Keep in the fridge until ready to use. Bring it out of the fridge at least 20–40 minutes before using. This butter also freezes well, so you could separate it into 2 logs and put one in the freezer for later use. This is delicious served with my fruit butters, such as the peach and thyme butter (pictured, see page 168).

For a dairy-free version, replace the butter with coconut oil (unmelted) or coconut butter—or try half coconut oil and half ghee instead.

Rose-scented yogurt.

SERVES 4-6

Amazing with fresh cantaloupe melon and a sprinkling of toasted almonds for breakfast, or with homemade granola and fresh raspberries.

Heaping 2 cups plain Greek or regular yogurt
½ teaspoon rose water

2 tablespoons light clear honey

Place all the ingredients in a bowl and mix gently until thoroughly combined.

Variation: Orange blossom yogurt
This is good with apple and polenta cakes, carrot cakes, citrus fruit salad, and maple toasted nuts.

Use 1 teaspoon orange blossom water in place of the rose water.

Ginger cream.

SERVES 4-6

Amazing with scones and damson jam, baked apples, poached plums, roasted plums, roast peaches, broiled peaches—in fact, any fruity dessert.

1¼ cups heavy cream
2 tablespoons plain yogurt

2 large pieces candied ginger, finely chopped
2 tablespoons syrup

Whip the cream with the yogurt in a medium bowl until you have a wonderful thick, smooth, and velvety consistency, being extremely careful not to overwhip it.

Add the ginger and syrup and fold through gently with a spatula or metal spoon, until the cream, when stirred, forms soft peaks. Use immediately.

Cinnamon crème fraîche.

SERVES 4-6

Delicious with baked apples, apple pie, stewed apples and buckwheat pancakes, apple and pear crumble. If crème fraîche is unavailable, substitute sour cream.

1 cup crème fraîche or sour cream
½ teaspoon ground cinnamon

⅓ cup light honey or maple syrup

Put all ingredients in a medium bowl, and gently mix until thoroughly combined.

Keep in a cool place until ready to serve.

Chantilly cream
(with a wild delicious twist).

SERVES 4-6

Chantilly cream is probably one of my favorite ways of serving cream. I can eat a bowl on my own; its softly peaking lusciousness transports me to heaven and beyond. You can sweeten it with whatever you like—honey or maple syrup work well—each adds their own unique flavor.

It's not traditional, but I love to add 1-2 tablespoons of unsweetened plain yogurt, for a hint of sourness that is offset by the sweetness of the cream. It also helps the cream not to become over-whipped. For me, most of the pleasure in whipped cream is its texture, so it should not go beyond that softly whipped stage, or "ribbon stage" as the professionals like to call it. Ribbon stage is reached when you can lift the whisk up, and the cream that falls gently off the end in a kind of ribbon, sits on top of the cream below for a minute, before it sinks back in.

You can use this cream to fill cakes, top puddings, tarts, pies, crêpes, and fresh or baked fruit, scones, and pikelets.

1¾ cups whipping cream or heavy cream
2 teaspoons raw honey
½ teaspoon vanilla extract

2 tablespoons unsweetened plain yogurt

Put all the ingredients in a mixing bowl. Whisk until the ribbon stage—when the cream is softly peaking and will only just hold its shape.

The cream will keep for a few days if covered well in the fridge.

Whipped coconut cream.

SERVES 4–6

This is a delicious, super-creamy, and dairy-free alternative to whipped cream. Use it as you would cream to decorate cakes, top crumbles, pies, and crêpes, or on fresh fruit salad. If you like, omit the vanilla, and try one of my sweet spice mixes from page 213.

2 x 14-ounce cans full-fat, additive-free coconut milk

1–2 teaspoons raw honey, maple syrup, or brown rice syrup
¼ teaspoon vanilla extract

Start by placing the cans of coconut milk upside down in the fridge, for at least 6 hours or overnight.

When they are thoroughly chilled, remove them from the fridge and turn them up the right way. Open both cans and pour out the liquid which will now be sitting on the top into a bowl. Set aside.

Scoop the solid cream into a separate large bowl.

Whip the solid cream, either by hand or with a hand-held mixer, until light and fluffy. If it's a bit solid and not creamy enough, add a little of the reserved liquid, a teaspoon or two at a time.

Lastly, add the raw honey and vanilla extract to taste.

This cream is best used immediately. It does keep in the fridge, but it will go hard again when chilled, so you may need to re-whip it when you want to use it.

Different brands of coconut milk can produce varying results. Some make far smoother cream than others.

Be sure to check the label and buy coconut milk that has no additives or emulsifying agents, such as tapioca starch in it, because this will prevent the cream from separating from the milk when you chill it, and it won't be possible to make whipped coconut cream.

Cashew mango cream.

MAKES 1 PINT JAR

This is another versatile concoction, delicious on so many things, including cakes, scones, puddings, crêpes, fresh fruit, granola, and chia pudding. It's dairy-free and loaded with flavor, fiber. and healthy fats, which make it filling and nutritious.

1 cup whole raw cashews, soaked for 6–7 hours, in filtered warm water with sea salt
3 ounces dried mango, soaked for about 2 hours in 1 cup near-boiling filtered water

¼ teaspoon vanilla extract, or ¼ vanilla bean, seeds scraped out
Small squeeze of fresh lime juice (optional)

Rinse the cashews under cold running water and leave to drain. Put the mango and its soaking water in a blender along with the drained cashews and vanilla seeds. Blend until completely smooth, add the lime juice, if using, and blend again. If the mixture seems too thick, add a little more water. Transfer the cream to a clean glass jam jar, allow to cool, and keep in the fridge where it will last for about four days until ready to use.

Rose cream.

MAKES ABOUT 1¼ CUPS

Try this in place of plain cream when sandwiching a Victoria sponge cake, or with fresh strawberries, stewed apples, fresh raspberries, gooseberry fool, apple crumble, apple cake, berry sponges, or little almond friands.

1¼ cups heavy cream
2 tablespoons plain yogurt

½ teaspoon rose water
3–4 tablespoons maple syrup

Rose water can vary a lot in strength, so start with ½ teaspoon and add more to taste if necessary.

Put all ingredients in a medium bowl, and whip the mixture until the cream forms soft peaks. Use immediately.

Sweet kefir cream.

SERVES 4–6

Sweet kefir cream is a little bit tangy, and a little bit naughty, and a whole lot delicious! You can feel justifiably virtuous eating it, too, because it's packed full of probiotics and vitamins, which makes it great for healing and nourishing the gut, and in turn the immune system. Kefir can be a bit of an acquired taste, but if you don't let it ferment for too long, the flavor is milder, therefore more suitable for sweet dishes. Try using it as a topping for scones alongside some of my heavenly chia jam, or on crêpes, puddings, cakes, and even tarts.

1 quantity of kefir cream (see page 122)
2 teaspoons raw honey, maple syrup, or brown rice syrup

½ teaspoon vanilla extract or one of my sweet spice mixes (see page 213)

To sweeten the kefir cream, gently fold through the honey and spices, so that you don't overwhip the cream. If it goes a little too stiff, add some plain yogurt to bring it back to a soft, creamy stage. Use immediately.

Basic nut milk

MAKES ABOUT 1 QUART

Nut milk is easy to make, and will keep well in the fridge for two to three days. It is a great and delicious alternative to cow's milk, and wonderful even if you don't have lactose allergies. There are many nutritional benefits to consuming nut milk, and depending on which nuts you choose, you will get different nutritional profiles.

EQUIPMENT

1 nut milk bag, or a large square of fine linen, muslin, or cheesecloth

5 ounces nuts (almonds, cashews, hazelnuts, pecans, brazil nuts, and macadamias—you can even add a handful of pumpkin or sunflower seeds), soaked overnight in filtered or spring water with a pinch of sea salt, or ¼ teaspoon raw apple cider vinegar, or 1 teaspoon lemon juice

1 quart warm, filtered, or spring water (warm but not hot)

Drain and rinse the nuts. Place them into a high speed blender along with the warm water. Blitz on high speed for about 2 minutes.

Place your nut milk bag or cheesecloth over a bowl, pour the milk through the nut milk bag, and lift up the cloth or bag, and allow the milk to drain through. Gently massage the rest of the liquid through until all the milk is in the bowl underneath, and only the pulp is left in the bag or cloth.

Pour the milk into a glass container, and allow to cool before transferring to the fridge to chill.

The pulp can be dried and used in baking in place of ground almonds.

To make raw honey and vanilla nut milk

This milk is totally delicious as a drink just as it is, or you can use it to add to smoothies, or as a base for hot chocolate or iced chocolate.

1 quart nut milk (made using cashews and almonds, see left for method)

2 tablespoons raw honey
1 teaspoon vanilla extract

When you have made the nut milk, warm it gently in a saucepan, and add the honey and vanilla extract, then stir to combine. When all the honey has dissolved, allow to cool before transferring to the fridge. Alternatively, blitz all the ingredients in a high-powered blender to incorporate the honey and vanilla extract.

To make Medjool date and cinnamon nut milk

This milk is totally delicious as a drink just as it is, or you can use it to add to smoothies or as a base for hot chocolate or iced chocolate.

1 quart nut milk (made using cashews and almonds, see left for method)

2–3 Medjool dates, pitted
1 teaspoon ground cinnamon

When you have made the nut milk, add the dates and cinnamon, then pour the milk along with the pitted dates and cinnamon back into the clean blender. Blitz until completely smooth. Pour into a clean glass jar, and keep in the fridge.

Matcha and hemp milk.

MAKES ABOUT 2 CUPS

Matcha is a super-powered powdered green tea. It gives a smooth and clear buzz, and is full of antioxidants. Hemp is full of proteins, and is an excellent source of essential fatty acids, including omega-3 and -6 and GLA in the perfect balance; it is also rich in vitamin E.

½ cup hemp hearts (seeds)	2 teaspoons Matcha powder
¾ cup unsweetened dried coconut	1–2 teaspoons raw honey, maple syrup, or brown rice syrup
2 cups filtered water, warmed	

Place the hemp hearts, coconut, and warm water into a high-speed blender. Blitz for 1–2 minutes, with a few pauses. Depending on your blender, it may take up to 3 minutes to get a good consistency.

Strain through a nut milk bag, or a piece of cheesecloth. Discard the solids, and pour the milk back into the blender, along with the Matcha and honey, then blitz until well-combined. Pour into a glass jar or bottle with a lid, and transfer to the fridge. Best served chilled.

Coconut milk.

MAKES ABOUT 2½ CUPS

Coconut milk is great for using as a base for smoothies or ice cream, or for putting in tea and coffee, and also for any of the following recipes in place of nut milk if you are allergic to nuts.

Scant 2½ cups just-boiled water	1½ cups coconut flakes

Place the water and flakes into a high-speed blender, allow it to stand for a few minutes, then blitz for a few minutes before straining through a cheesecloth or nut milk bag. Squeeze gently to get out all of the "milk". Keep the pulp—if you dry it out in a low oven you can use it as coconut flour in baking. Pour the strained coconut milk into a glass jar or bottle with a lid, and keep in the fridge.

Strawberry and sesame milk.

MAKES ABOUT 2 CUPS

This a delicious drink/smoothie. It's very nourishing and packed with enzymes, calcium, and vitamin C. A perfect little pick-me-up for the wee ones and adults alike.

4 tablespoons sesame seeds	2 cups filtered or spring water
1 cup almonds, soaked overnight, then rinsed and drained	1 teaspoon raw honey
	A small handful of frozen strawberries

Make the sesame and almond milk following the method for the basic nut milk (see page 178), using the sesame seeds, almonds, and filtered or spring water. When you have strained the milk, chill, then add it back to the blender, and blitz with the honey and strawberries. Keep in the fridge until ready to use.

Raw chocolate and hazelnut milk.

MAKES ABOUT 3¼ CUPS

This milk is best served cold and is delicious over ice. It's also great over granola, and as a base for banana and chocolate smoothies. You can also turn it into hot chocolate, by warming it in a pan, and sweetening to taste.

3 cups nut milk (made using 1 cup hazelnuts and 6 tablespoons unsweetened dried coconut, see basic nut milk on page 178 for method)	1 heaping tablespoon raw cacao powder
	2–3 teaspoons raw honey, or maple syrup
	A pinch of fine pink Himalayan sea salt

Make the nut milk according to the basic nut milk recipe. Add the warm hazelnut milk, and the rest of the ingredients to the blender, and blitz until everything is thoroughly combined. Transfer the milk to a glass bottle with a lid, and chill in the fridge.

Golden turmeric milk latte.

SERVES 2

This is a powerful anti-inflammatory, gut-healing, nourishing drink, great for healing a stressed digestive system. It's delicious, and is great to have before bedtime.

1¾ cups homemade coconut milk, whole cow's milk, or homemade almond milk (see basic nut milk recipe on page 178)

1 teaspoon turmeric or a knob of fresh turmeric, peeled

½ –1 teaspoon of ground cinnamon, to taste

1 teaspoon raw honey or maple syrup

A pinch of finely ground black pepper

A tiny piece of fresh ginger, peeled, about the size of a smallish coin

Place all the ingredients in a high-speed blender and blitz until completely smooth. Pour into a small saucepan, then heat for 4–6 minutes over medium heat, and simmer gently. Dust with a little extra cinnamon if you like before serving.

You can also put this hot milk mix into a French press and, while holding the lid on firmly, pull the plunger up and down a few times to froth the milk. Then pour the creamy latte into your favorite mug, dusted with cinnamon.

Drink immediately.

Dairy-free custard.

SERVES 6

This is a great alternative to milk custard; velvety and glorious, just as any custard should be. You can make it as vanilla or chocolate custard simply by adding the different flavorings to the base recipe.

2½ cups almond milk, or a combo of almond and cashew milk, or coconut milk (see pages 178 and 180 for my nut milk and coconut milk recipes)

1 teaspoon vanilla extract or 1 vanilla bean, seeds scraped out (or, for

chocolate custard, omit the vanilla and add 2 heaping teaspoons raw cacao powder)

1½ tablespoons honey or 2 tablespoons maple syrup

2 whole eggs and 1 egg yolk

1 tablespoon cornstarch

Set a medium saucepan over medium–high heat, and pour in the milk, vanilla or cacao powder, and your sweetener of choice.

While the milk is heating, crack the eggs into a medium bowl, add the cornstarch, and whisk until thoroughly combined. Keep stirring the milk on the stovetop, and when it's nearly boiling, remove from the heat, and slowly pour it over the egg mix, whisking vigorously all the time.

Now pour it all back into the saucepan, and return it to medium heat—not too hot, or the mixture will split. Stir the custard continuously with a wooden spoon as it cooks. It will gradually thicken with the heat—keep stirring so that it doesn't curdle.

When the custard is done, it should coat the back of the wooden spoon. Pour the custard into a glass pitcher. Serve hot or cold.

If there are any lumps, you can pour the mix through a fine-mesh strainer.

If you want to serve the custard cold, place a piece of plastic wrap directly over the top of the custard so that it has full contact—this will prevent a skin from forming.

Vanilla custard.

SERVES 6

Luscious and delightfully creamy, this custard is amazing on fruit pies, puddings, cakes, and caramelized bananas.

½ vanilla bean
2½ cups whole milk

4 extra-large egg yolks
3–4 tablespoons maple syrup

Put the vanilla bean and milk in a medium saucepan, and bring slowly to a boil. Just before it starts to bubble, remove from the heat.

Whisk the egg yolks and maple syrup in a large bowl.

Remove the vanilla bean from the hot milk, and slowly pour the milk into the egg yolk mix, whisking all the time.

Use the tip of a sharp knife to split open the vanilla bean, and scrape out the seeds into the custard mixture.

Return the mixture to the pan, and stir over gentle heat until the mixture thickens enough to coat the back of a spoon. Be very careful not to allow the mixture to boil, or it will split.

Once the custard has reached the desired thickness, pour the custard into a cool pitcher or pouring bowl (if you leave the custard in the pan even away from the heat, it can still split from the residual heat at the base of the pan).

Stir occasionally with a wooden spoon to prevent a skin forming.

Serve warm or cold.

Dark chocolate custard.

SERVES 6

Wonderful on caramelized bananas, banana cake, roasted pears or peaches, and any kind of crumbly spongy pudding.

2½ cups whole milk
4 extra-large egg yolks
3 tablespoons maple syrup

7 ounces good-quality dark chocolate, finely chopped

Put the milk in a medium saucepan, bring slowly to a boil, then remove from the heat and set aside.

Whisk the egg yolks and maple syrup in a large bowl. Slowly pour the hot milk into the egg mixture, whisking all the time, then add the chocolate. Return the mixture to the pan, and stir over gentle heat until the custard thickens enough to coat the back of a spoon.Remove from the heat, and pour into a cool pitcher or pouring bowl. Stir occasionally to prevent a skin forming. Serve warm or cold.

Strawberry and vanilla chia jam.

MAKES 1 PINT JAR

Chia jam provides an excellent and delicious way of getting more of these super seeds into your daily diet. It's really easy to make, and it uses less sugar than the more traditional jam recipes. It doesn't last as long, but it will keep in the fridge for a good week. I use it for decorating cakes, topping nut butter on toast, swirling through slow-cooked porridge with yogurt, on cookies, and mixed with granola with fresh fruit and coconut yogurt. Chia seeds are one of the most nutritious foods on the planet, loaded with fiber, protein, omega-3 fatty acids, and various micronutrients. What's not to love?

7 ounces strawberries, fresh or frozen	Squeeze of lemon juice
2 tablespoons honey, or more if desired	½ teaspoon vanilla extract
	½ tablespoon chia seeds

Put the strawberries, honey, and vanilla in a small saucepan over medium heat, and add 1–2 tablespoons of water, just enough to get them to release their juices. As they start to bubble, simmer on low for about 10 minutes. Remove from the heat, and allow to cool. Add the chia seeds, and stir to prevent any lumps from forming. Leave the mix to stand for another couple of minutes, then stir again. Repeat this three or four times. Pour the jam into a clean glass jar, and transfer to the fridge for several hours or overnight to thicken up and chill. This jam will keep for about 10 days in the fridge.

Variation: Raspberry and rose chia jam
Replace the strawberries with raspberries and use ½ teaspoon of rose water instead of the vanilla.

Raw goji, orange, and cardamom chia jam.

MAKES 1 PINT JAR

This jam will last for about a week in the fridge, and it also freezes well. It's great on hot buttered toast, or layered up with granola and yogurt, or served with cheese as an accompaniment.

2 whole unwaxed oranges	2 cardamom pods, seeds only, finely ground
3 tablespoons raw honey, more to taste if you like	3 tablespoons chia seeds
¾ cup goji berries, soaked in water for 4 hours and drained	Sea salt

Grate the zest from the oranges using a very fine zester or grater (a microplane works best). You need 1 teaspoon of compacted zest.

Peel the oranges, removing the pith and any seeds, then pulse the orange flesh in a food processor or blender along with the zest, honey, cardamom, and a tiny pinch of salt until smooth.

Add the goji berries and chia seeds to the blended orange mixture, stir, and leave for about 15 minutes.

Pulse the mixture a couple of times, so that the goji berries are blended in, but still chunky—you may need to pulse a couple more times.

Pour the mixture into a glass jar, and transfer to the fridge to set overnight.

SWEET PANTRY Sweet Butters and Creams Nut Milks and Custard *Jams and Curds* Chocolate

Honey and lemon curd.

Lemon curd is a most luscious and decadent thing. It's beautiful in tarts, as a topping for crêpes, on French toast, and on yogurt and fruit. Use it for the parfait recipe, right—it's a cinch to throw together, and is a perfect way to end a late summery Sunday lunch.

Finely grated zest and juice of 6 unwaxed lemons

1 scant cup light honey

1¼ sticks cold butter, cubed

4 large eggs and 1–2 large egg yolks

Begin by sterilizing several glass jars, either by putting them and the lids through the dishwasher, or by boiling them in a pan of water for 10 minutes.

Place the lemon zest, juice, honey, and butter into a medium heatproof bowl. Place the bowl over a pot of barely simmering water, making sure the base of the bowl doesn't touch the water. Allow the ingredients to melt and come together, helping this process along a little by stirring with a whisk every so often.

In a separate bowl, give the eggs a thorough beating with a metal whisk. Slowly pour the eggs into the lemon mix and stir continuously for 9–10 minutes, or until the mix is custard-like, beautifully thick, and irresistible.

When the curd is ready, remove it from the heat, and set aside, but do give it a little stir every now and then as it cools, to keep a skin from forming. Scrape the lemon curd into sterilized jars and seal. It will keep for several weeks in the fridge.

OPTIONAL ADDITIONS

Add ¼–½ teaspoon rose water to make lemon and rose curd.
Add ¼ teaspoon vanilla extract to make lemon and vanilla curd.

Lemon curd, rose, and clementine parfait.

Homemade meringues give you the ideal combination: crisp outside and a chewy center.

EQUIPMENT

9 x 5-inch loaf pan, lined loosely with plastic wrap or waxed paper

2¾ cups heavy cream

1 teaspoon rose water

2 tablespoons raw honey or maple syrup

7 ounces meringues (see page 210), lightly broken up into pieces

10 heaping tablespoons lemon curd (see left)

Grated zest of 4 clementines

Before you begin, place a mixing bowl into the fridge to chill for 30 minutes to 1 hour before using.

Place the heavy cream, rose water, and honey into the pre-chilled mixing bowl, and whisk until soft peaks form. You want it thick and soft, with the cream just holding its shape, with no stiff peaks whatsoever. Don't be tempted to go too far—over-whipped cream is not what you want here. Soft and luscious is key!

Add the meringues and lemon curd, then grate in the clementine zest. Give the whole mixture a gentle fold to combine all the elements. You want distinct marbled layers. Be very careful not to overmix.

Using a soft spatula, carefully scrape the mixture into the prepared pan, cover lightly with a piece of baking parchment, then pop into the freezer for 4–5 hours, or overnight, until set. The parfait will last for several days in the freezer, but do take it out at least 20 minutes before serving to soften a little.

To serve, lift the parfait up and out of its pan and slice. Serve just as it is, or with a scattering of fresh rose petals and fresh mint tea.

Raw peach and ginger
no-cook jam

MAKES 1 PINT JAR

This is a super-simple and delicious jam, great for topping crêpes, toast, granola, and yogurt. You could also use it to layer chia pudding pots, or add it to crumbles and pies. In New Zealand I get these wonderful big dried peaches, but if you can't find them, just use unsulfured dried apricots.

Scant 1¼ pounds dried peaches or
  apricots (or both)
⅔ cup raw, light honey (or brown rice
  syrup or maple syrup)
1–2 tablespoons lemon juice (start with 1,
  and add more to taste)

¼ teaspoon ground ginger
or ½ vanilla bean, seeds scraped out
  (keep the empty bean for scenting
  coconut sugar or adding to stewed
  fruit)
A tiny pinch of pink Himalayan sea salt

Start by placing the peaches in a glass or ceramic bowl. Pour over enough very hot water to completely submerge the dried fruit, and place a plate over the top to cover them and hold in the warmth. Leave the fruit to soak for at least a few hours, or overnight.

When the peaches have rehydrated, and become plump and juicy, drain them thoroughly, discarding the soaking liquor, and pop the fruit into a high-speed blender, or food processor.

To the blender add the honey, 1 tablespoon of lemon juice, the ginger or vanilla, and the salt, and blitz until you have a lovely smooth jam-like consistency. You can leave it a little chunky if you prefer—some texture is no bad thing. If your jam is too stiff, and not blending well, simply add a little water, a tiny amount at a time, to loosen the mix.

At this point taste the jam. If you think it needs more lemon juice or more spices, add more to taste. When you are happy that the flavors are balanced, scrape your beautiful homemade jam into some clean glass jars, and keep in the fridge.

This delicious fruit jam will keep for one week or up to 10 days if kept chilled.

My classic
dark, raw chocolate.

MAKES ABOUT 9 OUNCES

This raw, dark chocolate can be made and eaten as it is or used as a base for other recipes, such as the fruit and nut wheel on page 190, served warm as a raw chocolate fondue, or drizzled over ice cream, fresh fruit, caramelized bananas or crêpes. Raw cacao has multiple health benefits, so no need to feel guilty when eating this. It is packed full of antioxidants and good fats, which make our skin glow, and support brain and metabolic health.

EQUIPMENT	8 ounces cacao butter
Cooking thermometer	4 tablespoons coconut oil
(not essential but	4 heaping tablespoons raw
recommended)	cacao powder
Silicone chocolate molds	4 tablespoons raw honey,
or a baking sheet lined with	maple syrup, or brown
silicone paper	rice syrup

Put about 1¼ inches of water in a small saucepan, and set over low heat. Place a bowl on top of the pan that fits snugly over the top without the base of it touching the water. Put the cacao butter and coconut oil into the bowl, and very slowly melt the butter. Check the temperature and don't allow the mix to go higher than 104–113°F; if you think it's going to get hotter than that and some of the butter hasn't melted, take the bowl off the heat and allow the residual heat to melt the butter.

When the butter/oil mix has fully melted and is at that critical 104–113°F, measure in the cacao powder and raw honey. Whisk until the mixture is completely and thoroughly emulsified, and the temperature has come down to 84–86°F. You need to mix it well at this stage, otherwise it will separate, so mix until it looks beautifully smooth and glossy. However, do be careful not to over-mix, or the chocolate can stiffen. If this happens, pop the bowl back over the heat, and stir for a few moments until it relaxes again.

When the chocolate is ready and it is around that 84–86°F mark, pour the mix into the molds, or lined sheet, and pop into the fridge to set. Once it has set, either pop the chocolate out of the molds or break it up from the tray. I find it melts easily, so I put mine in a glass jar in the fridge, where it will keep well for up to three months.

Fig, date, and apricot
salted caramel chocolates.

MAKES ABOUT 20

These gorgeous little treats are a great way to use my raw chocolate.

1 quantity of My classic dark	10 dried figs, hard stems
raw chocolate (see left),	removed
still liquid	10 Medjool dates, pitted
10 unsulfured dried apricots	Sea salt flakes

Line a baking sheet with silicone paper. Prepare the raw chocolate until the point where it is smooth and glossy.

Put the dried fruit in a high-powered blender or food processor, and blitz until you have a thick paste.

Take little teaspoonfuls of the mix, and roll into small balls with damp hands, laying them on the prepared baking sheet as you go. Next, use a skewer or cake fork to dip them into the cooled liquid raw chocolate, transfer back to the sheet, and sprinkle each ball with a few flakes of sea salt—not too much. When all the balls are rolled, dipped, and sprinkled with salt, put the sheet in the freezer. If the chocolate is melting off the balls, keep the sheet in the freezer, and freeze as you go.

Raw chocolate
nut butter cups and
Raw chocolate chia jam cups.

MAKES 12

These heavenly little raw chocolate, chia jam, and nut butter cups are so delicious, and are packed with healthy fats, protein, and energy-boosting goodness. They do require a few different elements coming together, but the end result is divine. Little ones enjoy helping with the stirring (and bowl licking!).

2–3 quantities My classic
  dark, raw chocolate (see
  page 189), still warm
1 quantity of your favorite
  nut butter (see page
  113—roasted almonds and

cashews with maple syrup
  would be incredible!)
1 quantity of your favorite
  chia jam (see pages
  187–188)

Line a 12-hole cupcake pan with paper cases. Pour some of the warm raw chocolate into the paper cases to a depth of about 2 inches, then put the pan in the freezer for 20 minutes to harden the chocolate. Take the pan out of the freezer, and pop a teaspoonful of nut butter onto the center of six of the chocolate-filled cases, then do the same with the chia jam onto the remaining six cases. Flatten the butter and jam a little, but try to keep it in the center of the cases. Now pour more chocolate over the top, so that the nut butter and chia jam are completely covered, and the tops are flat. Pop back into the freezer for an additional 30 minutes, or until completely set.

Keep refrigerated until ready to eat.

Fruit and nut raw dark
chocolate wheel with rose
and bee pollen.

SERVES AT LEAST 20

This is my grown-up, healthy take on an after dinner chocolate. It's best served in delicate little slices. It's a super-intense hit of raw chocolate, and the different textures from the nuts and dried fruit give it a pleasing crunch to contrast with the velvety smooth pollen on top. The rose petals are pure whimsy, but worth it for the visual pleasure.

2 quantities My classic
  dark, raw chocolate (see
  page 189)
1 teaspoon vanilla extract
4 tablespoons tahini
8 Medjool dates, pitted and
  chopped
⅔ cup brazil nuts, chopped

⅔ cup lightly roasted
  almonds, chopped

TO DECORATE
2 tablespoons bee pollen
A few generous pinches of
  dried rose petals (optional)

Line an 8-inch round cake pan with silicone paper. Follow the instructions for making the dark raw chocolate to the point where you have added the cacao powder and honey, and mixed until it is smooth and glossy. Mix in the tahini, then add the dates and nuts.

Pour into the prepared pan and refrigerate. When the chocolate is just setting, remove the pan from the fridge, and sprinkle over the bee pollen and rose petals, then pop it back in the fridge to set fully.

I like to keep this raw chocolate wheel in the fridge, and just take it out and cut off thin pieces when I feel like a treat with my afternoon tea. It makes a lovely after-supper treat to serve with peppermint tea or coffee if you're having a dinner party.

Homemade gut-loving gelatin.

SERVES 4

Love it or hate it, gelatin can be nutritious and wonderfully delightful. It can be childish, in a good way of course, but it can also be sexy and grown-up. Homemade gelatin is far cry from the overly sweet and terribly flavored store-bought stuff. Providing homemade gelatin is made with good-quality powdered gelatin, it can also be incredibly good for you in numerous ways (see page 202 for more information).

FOUNDATION GELATIN MIX	3 tablespoons grass-fed
1 quart liquid (see flavor options right)	gelatin (this gives a soft set; if you like it really firm, add 1 more tablespoon)

To make the gelatin

Choose which flavor you want to make from the flavoring suggestions, and pour the liquid into a small saucepan. Stir well to combine. Sprinkle the gelatin over the cold liquid and stir.

Allow it to sit for 5 minutes—this gives the gelatin time to bloom. Place the saucepan over medium heat, and bring the liquid up to quite a hot temperature, but NOT boiling. Boiling the liquid will destroy the setting agents in the gelatin.

When the liquid is hot, give it a really good stir to fully dissolve the gelatin. Try to stir the liquid gently and not whisk it, as you don't want lots of foam on the top of the gelatin.

If you have made foam, you can scoop it off with a small fine-mesh strainer. Take the pan off the heat and pour the gelatin into four equal-sized molds (I like to use ramekins) or one big bowl. Pop the molds into the fridge to set—this will take about 2 hours (longer if setting the gelatin in a big bowl). When you are ready to serve the gelatin, just pop the molds into a bowl of very hot water for a few seconds, and then turn the gelatin out onto a dessert plate, and serve with cream or fruit.

FLAVORING SUGGESTIONS

To make rhubarb gelatin with rose cream.

For the liquid: ¾ cup rhubarb, rose, and lime syrup (see page 217) and 3¼ cups filtered water. Serve with rose cream (see page 174).

To make blackberry gelatin with warm apple compote and chantilly cream.

For the liquid: ¾ cup blueberry and blackberry syrup (see page 218) and 3¼ cups filtered water. Serve with warm apple compote and chantilly cream (see page 173).

To make grape gelatin.

For the liquid: 1 cup water and 3 cups grape juice.

To make coconut gelatin with fresh mango and coconut cream.

For the liquid: 1 quart coconut water. You may not need all 3 tablespoons of honey—adjust to taste. Serve with slices of fresh mango and my coconut cream (see page 174).

To make elderflower gelatin with white peaches.

For the liquid: ¾ cup elderflower syrup and 3¼ cups filtered water. You will also need 2–3 white peaches, sliced in half, pits removed, and each half cut into five slices. Lay the peach slices in the bottom of each glass before pouring in the gelatin to set. Sprinkle over some elderflowers when serving. This gelatin is also delicious with chantilly cream (see page 173), or rose cream (see page 174).

SWEET PANTRY Sweet Butters and Creams Nut Milks and Custard Jams and Curds Chocolate

Fluffy gut-loving marshmallows.

SERVES 4-6

What could be more wonderful than homemade marshmallows? These are super-easy to make, and great for gut health. You can mix and match the flavors depending on what you might fancy. They are not great for toasting, though, as fresh marshmallows melt too quickly, and fall off the stick. Still, they are delicious, and such a treat—and a healthy one at that if you're using grass-fed gelatin (see page 202 for more information).

4 tablespoons grass-fed gelatin powder	¾ cup maple syrup or coconut nectar
1⅓ cup filtered or spring water	¼ teaspoon sea salt

Line an 8-inch square baking pan with parchment paper lengthwise and then, using another piece, line widthwise, ensuring there is enough parchment paper overhanging the sides to cover the marshmallows.

Place the gelatin and 5½ fluid ounces of water in a freestanding mixer, and mix until lovely and soft. This will take a few minutes, which also allows time for the gelatin to bloom.

While the gelatin and water are mixing, pour the remaining water into a saucepan with your sweetener of choice, along with the salt, and bring the mixture to a boil. Gently boil for 7–9 minutes, or until the mix reaches roughly 240°F, then take off the heat.

Turn the freestanding mixer with the bloomed gelatin in it to its lowest setting, and very slowly pour the sweetened syrup mixture into the bowl. Once all the syrup has been added, turn the mixer up to high and continue beating for 8–10 minutes, or until the mixture becomes voluminous, thick, and fluffy. Don't be tempted to keep beating once it has reached this stage, or the mixture will become impossible to spread into the pan. At this point you can add different flavors or just keep it plain—see options, right.

After you have added your flavorings (if using), turn off the mixer and transfer the marshmallow fluff to the prepared pan. Using a palette knife or the back of a spoon, even out the top of the marshmallow fluff to create a nice even top. Set aside, and leave for about 1 hour until the marshmallow is completely set.

Once set, cut into bite-sized cubes, and dust with raw cacao powder, freeze-dried raspberry powder, or GM-free cornstarch.

FLAVORING SUGGESTIONS

Vanilla and chocolate.

Add 1 teaspoon of vanilla extract to the mix before you scrape it into the pan. Dust the finished marshmallows in raw cacao powder.

Double chocolate.

Add 2 teaspoons sifted raw cacao powder to the mixture and fold through until well combined, before scraping into the pan to set. Dust the set and cubed marshmallows in raw cacao powder.

Raspberry.

Fold a handful of fresh or crushed freeze-dried raspberries through the mixture before scraping into the pan. Dust with unrefined confectioners' sugar or cornstarch, raw cacao powder, or freeze-dried raspberry powder.

Lemon and rose.

Add 5 drops of food-grade lemon essential oil, or the zest of ½ an unwaxed lemon and 1 teaspoon of rose water to the mix. Thoroughly combine before scraping into the pan to set. Dust the marshmallows with GM-free cornstarch, or unrefined confectioners' sugar.

Orange blossom and pistachio.

Add 1 teaspoon of orange blossom water and a small handful of roughly chopped pistachios to the fluffy mix, and fold through before scraping into the pan to set. Once the marshmallows have set, cut into cubes and dust with GM-free cornstarch, unrefined confectioners' sugar or raw cacao powder.

Nice cream.

SERVES 2-3

Nice cream is ice cream, but not in the traditional sense. It doesn't have any dairy, it takes mere moments to make, and has the consistency of a soft-scoop ice cream. It's highly nutritious, especially when made using seasonal dark berries and raw honey. I love making this on a hot summer's day. My son particularly enjoys it when I use just frozen berries; it's like beautifully soft berry sorbet.

---

4 bananas, sliced and frozen

7 tablespoons almond milk (see page 178)

2 tablespoons raw honey or maple syrup

½–1 teaspoon vanilla extract (optional)

Simply place the frozen banana slices into a high-speed blender (such as a Vitamix), add the milk and syrup, and blend, using the tamper to push the bananas down as it blends.

Keep going until you have perfectly smooth soft-scoop banana ice cream.

You can make many variations of this ice cream; all are delicious, and just as easy to make.

To make Ferrero Rocher-flavored nice cream:
First, make caramelized hazelnuts by toasting whole blanched nuts in a heavy-bottomed skillet along with 1–2 tablespoons of maple syrup, depending on how many nuts you are toasting, and stir until the syrup has all but disappeared and turned thick, golden, and toffee-like. It easily turns into burnt sugar, so watch it carefully. When the nuts are done, remove them from the pan and allow to cool—the syrup should harden into toffee as they cool. Chop into pieces.

Make nice cream using hazelnut milk in place of almond milk, and maple syrup in place of honey. Add 3 tablespoons of raw cacao powder and top with the chopped caramelized hazelnuts.

To make a very berry summer nice cream:
Use half frozen banana and half frozen berries, either a mix of berries or just one sort will do—strawberries or raspberries, black or red currants, or even blackberries and elderberries.

Vanilla and honey ice cream
(with seasonal variations).

SERVES 3-4

2 teaspoons vanilla extract or 2 vanilla
  beans, seeds and scrapped beans
2⅓ cups heavy cream

3 tablespoons light honey
3 egg yolks

Start by adding the vanilla extract (or beans without the seeds if using), cream, and honey to a saucepan. Place it over medium heat, stirring often. In a separate bowl, whisk the egg yolks. When the cream mixture is nearly boiling, take it off the heat, and slowly pour it over the yolks, whisking as you go, so as to prevent the yolks from scrambling.

When you have added all the cream mixture to the yolks, add the seeds from the beans, if using. Pour the mixture back into the saucepan, place over low–medium heat, and stir until lightly thickened.

Take off the heat, and pour the mixture into a bowl or pitcher to cool. If you leave the mixture in the pot, it can curdle from the residual heat. When the custard base has cooled, pour the mixture into an ice-cream maker, and churn until set.

At this stage you can eat it immediately, or you can pop the ice cream into a freezerproof container, and freeze for later.

For a fruit swirl and extra flavor, try any of the following: Blackberry purée, raspberry purée, Strawberry purée, Roasted peach purée, Roasted plum purée, Roasted rhubarb purée, maple caramelized pear purée or any of the fruit coulis from page 215. Simply swirl the fruit purée into the ice cream before freezing.

To make a toasted nut and vanilla ice cream:
Toast a handful of nuts—almonds, pecans, or hazelnuts would work well—then remove the skins, and chop roughly. Mix into the ice cream before freezing.

SWEET PANTRY Sweet Butters and Creams Nut Milks and Custard Jams and Curds Chocolate

Chia pudding.

SERVES 4-6

Chia seeds may be tiny, but they are one of the most nutritious foods on the planet. I never tire of chia pudding for breakfast, especially in the warmer months. Once you have made the basic mix, you can top it with anything you like. I love adding some kefir to the mix for added gut-healing, immune-boosting probiotics. This chia pudding will last for at least a week in the fridge, so you can make up a batch, and then just use a little each morning in your breakfast as and when you like.

BASIC CHIA PUDDING MIX

2 cups coconut milk or almond milk, or a mix of the two (see pages 178 and 180)

2 tablespoons raw honey

4 tablespoons chia seeds

½–1 teaspoon vanilla extract (optional)

½–1 teaspoon ground cinnamon (optional)

1–2 tablespoons kefir (see page 120), either milk or coconut (optional)

Pour the coconut/almond milk into a glass jar, add the raw honey, and give it a good whisk. Add the chia seeds, and use a fork to stir them through the milk really well. Let the mix stand for 1–2 minutes, and then stir it really well again, breaking up any lumps that have formed. Repeat this process a few times over a 10-minute period. Add the spices, if using, and stir. Place the chia pudding in the fridge, and let it soak overnight, or for at least a few hours. This allows the chia seeds to soak and thicken up.

Layered vanilla chia and fruit cup.

1 quantity of the basic chia mix

1¼ pounds of your favorite fresh fruit or compote

Edible flowers, optional

Spoon half the chia mix into three glasses. Sprinkle over half the fruit, layer on more chia pudding, then sprinkle over the rest of the fruit. Serve.

Raw chocolate and red berry chia pudding.

MADE IN ADVANCE

1 quantity of the basic chia mix, to which add 1 tablespoon raw cacao powder before soaking, and 2 tablespoons maple syrup, or raw clear honey

FOR ASSEMBLING

12 ounces strawberries and raspberries, mixed

Juice of ½ lemon

1½ teaspoons coconut sugar

1 tablespoon cacao nibs

1–2 spoonfuls coconut kefir (optional)

Put the berries, lemon juice, and coconut sugar in a small bowl, and mix well, lightly crushing the raspberries. Allow the mixture to stand for 10 minutes.

Spoon half the chocolate chia pudding into three glasses, spoon over half the macerated berries, then layer the rest of the chocolate chia pudding on top. Finish with the rest of the berries, and lastly sprinkle over the cacao nibs. Serve.

You can also use coconut water as the liquid base, but I like my pudding creamy and with plenty of healthy fats, which help you to feel full, and maintain your energy levels.

For an extra boost of flavor and gut-loving probiotics, use 1½ cups of coconut milk and ½ cup of kefir.

Add 1-2 teaspoons of one of the sweet spice mixes from page 213 for extra flavor.

Pannacotta.

SERVES 4

Pannacotta has to be one of my all-time favorite desserts. It's perfect at any time of the year, served up with whatever fruit happens to be in season. Make sure you don't overdo the gelatin, or you will end up with a hard, rubbery dessert instead of a soft, sexy, wobbly one. It's a tough choice, but I think I prefer the coconut version—although both are totally amazing.

1⅔ cups full-fat coconut milk or 1¼ cups heavy cream plus 6 tablespoons milk, mixed together	1¼ teaspoons grass-fed gelatin
	½ vanilla bean, seeds only, or ⅓ teaspoon vanilla extract
	¼–⅓ cup maple syrup

Pour half the milk into a saucepan, add the gelatin, and give it a good whisk, then set aside for 5 minutes to allow to bloom.

Add the vanilla, then gently warm the mixture over medium heat, whisking thoroughly to dissolve the gelatin. Do not let the mix boil, or you will destroy the setting ability of the gelatin.

When the gelatin has dissolved, and the mix is warm to hot, remove from the heat, and add the rest of the milk, stirring thoroughly. Add the maple syrup to taste (start with ¼ cup and taste the mix, then add a little more if needed). I prefer my pannacotta not too sweet, but it depends what you are serving it with.

Pour the mixture into four little molds or teacups, and place in the fridge to set for 4 hours or overnight.

To serve, dip the molds into very hot water for a few seconds, then turn the pannacotta upside-down onto a dessert plate, remove the mold, and serve drizzled with fresh or cooked fruit. You could also serve with the Blueberry and maple sauce on page 215, or my Honey salted caramel sauce (see page 214), and fresh raspberries.

Other seasonal ideas:
Roasted rhubarb and vanilla, poached cherries with some of the syrup, roasted strawberries drizzled with a little maple syrup or dessert wine before roasting, fresh or roasted plums with some of the juice from the roasting pan, fresh or bottled feijoas (pineapple guavas) or fresh pineapple salsa (goes beautifully with the coconut pannacotta).

A word about good quality-gelatin.

The gelatin I use in my pannacotta, marshmallow, and gelatin recipes comes from really good-quality, grass-fed animals. This can be a lot more expensive to buy than ordinary gelatin, but its nutritional benefits far outweigh its price tag—plus it usually comes in really large tubs, so it lasts ages. Good-quality gelatin is incredibly gut healing, and contains amazing skin healing properties, making it great as an anti-aging ingredient, due to its collagen content. It is great for teeth, hair, and nails, and also stretch marks and cellulite, due to the essential amino acids such as glycine, and the protein it contains. Glycine and protein are also effective at detoxing the liver, helping with weight loss, and aiding digestion, making it great for helping with issues like leaky gut. Gelatin also contains easy-to-digest calcium, phosphorus, silicon, sulfur, and trace minerals, which help to build a healthy bone matrix. Gelatin also helps with arthritis, as it contains chondroitin, which has long been used as a supplement for people with arthritis, joint pain, and stiffness. The chondroitin found in gelatin supports joints, cartilage, and tendons. Good-quality gelatin supports a healthy metabolism, due to the essential amino acids it contains. These also help regulate insulin sensitivity, which helps prevent abdominal fat storage. Grass-fed gelatin also helps our adrenals, which in turn helps us to deal with stress and cortisol levels. It also helps to balance hormone levels, repair muscles, lower inflammation within the body, and lessen allergies. Wow—it seriously packs a punch in the health department! So start making all the marshmallows, pannacotta, and "gummies" you fancy.

The perfect all-in-one sponge cake.

MAKES 1 8-INCH CAKE

This is my fail-safe recipe for whipping up a light and airy sponge cake for birthday cakes and afternoon tea parties. It's super-easy, and spelt is a great alternative to all-purpose white flour: it contains far less gluten, and it tastes wonderful. Spelt is a heritage grain, and much easier to digest than some of the more modern varieties. Once you get the hang of the basic sponge, you can then decorate the cake any way you like from the suggestions on page 206, depending on the season. I love having basic recipes that can be adapted throughout the year—it takes the stress out of planning. This is my son's absolute favorite cake; the one he always requests when his birthday rolls around in the middle of summer.

2¾ sticks unsalted butter, well softened, but not melted

3 cups white spelt flour, sifted

5 extra-large free-range eggs

2½ teaspoons baking powder

1⅛ cups coconut sugar

Scant ½ cup honey

1½ teaspoons vanilla extract

3–4 tablespoons whole milk

To make the recipe lactose-free, use ghee in place of butter, and nut milk in place of whole milk .

To make it gluten-free, substitute the spelt for a gluten-free flour blend, and add 1 teaspoon of xanthum gum.

Preheat the oven to 400°F. Line two 8-inch round layer cake pans with butter and baking parchment, or one 8-inch loose-bottomed deep round cake pan.

Place all the ingredients into a free-standing mixing bowl, and beat for a few minutes until thoroughly combined, smooth, creamy, and fluffy. If you don't have a free-standing mixer, you can use a hand-held electric whisk on the low–medium setting.

If using layer cake pans, scrape the batter equally into both pans, even out the mixture using a palette knife, or the back of a spoon, and put into the preheated oven on the middle shelf. Bake for about 20 minutes, or until the cakes are golden and spring back to the touch.

If using an 8-inch loose-bottomed cake pan, scrape all the batter into the pan, level the surface, and put into the preheated oven on the middle shelf. Bake for 40 minutes, or until golden, and the center springs back to the touch. You can also test doneness by inserting a skewer into the middle of the cake: if it comes out clean, then the cake is ready.

Take the cake(s) out of the oven and set aside to cool for 10 minutes before removing them from the pan(s) and placing on a wire rack to cool completely.

If you have baked the cake in one pan, this is the moment to cut it in half, once it has cooled, and you are ready to frost the cake (see page 206).

The perfect sponge cake
(continued).

SEASONAL DECORATING SUGGESTIONS

Spring: Rhubarb, pomegranate, and rose.

You will need 1 quantity of Chantilly cream (page 173), and add 1 teaspoon of rose water to the cream when whipping.

Preheat the oven to 350°F. Cut 4–5 slender stalks of pink forced rhubarb into 2½-inch pieces, and lay them in a single layer in a roasting dish just big enough to hold them. Drizzle with a scant ½ cup honey or maple syrup, and a few tablespoons of water, and cover. Roast for 15–20 minutes, or until soft, but still holding their shape.

Remove from the oven, and allow to cool. Lay the base cake layer on a serving platter, spoon over a generous amount of rhubarb jam, then spoon over the rose water, Chantilly cream, and lastly spoon over the rhubarb and syrup. Top with rose petals, and scatter with the seeds of half a pomegranate.

Summer: Summer berries and vanilla chia jam, with vanilla Chantilly cream.

You will need 1 quantity of Chantilly cream (see page 173), and add 1 teaspoon of vanilla and coconut sugar spice mix (page 213) to the cream when whipping. You will also need 1 quantity of my raspberry and rose chia jam (see page 185).

Lay the base cake layer onto a serving platter, spoon over the Chantilly cream, then the chia jam, just enough to cover the cream in generous amount.

Lastly, scatter with 7 ounces of summer berries; strawberries, and raspberries, any lovely fresh berries are a treat. Top with the second layer of cake, give a light dusting of unrefined confectioners' sugar and decorate with a beautiful garden rose if you have one available.

Autumn: Roasted plums and spiced cream with hazelnuts.

You will need 1 quantity of Chantilly cream (see page 173), and add ¼ teaspoon vanilla extract to the cream when whipping.

Preheat the oven to 350°F. Take 4 large red plums, or 8 smaller plums, cut in half, and remove the pits, lay them cut-side up in a single layer in a roasting pan just big enough to hold them. Place a small knob of butter or coconut oil in the center of each plum, sprinkle with 4 teaspoons of my vanilla, star anise, nutmeg, and cinnamon spice mix (see page 213). Roast for 15 minutes, or until tender and sizzling, and catching at the edges. Set aside to cool. Roast ⅔ cup hazelnuts on a baking sheet for 8 minutes, rub them in a napkin to remove the skins, then chop roughly. Lay the base cake layer on a serving platter, generously spoon over the cream, then arrange the plums on top and drizzle over any juices. Lastly, scatter over the gloriously golden toasted hazelnuts. Top with the second cake layer and dust with unrefined confectioners' sugar.

Winter: Honey lemon curd with toasted almonds.

You will need 1 quantity of Chantilly cream (see page 173), 1 quantity of my honey and lemon curd (see page 187) and 1 cup toasted flaked almonds.

Lay the base cake layer on a serving platter, spoon over first the cream, then the curd, and sprinkle with the toasted flaked almonds for a wonderful crunch. Top with the second layer of sponge, and dust lightly with unrefined confectioners' sugar.

The world's best buckwheat brownies.

MAKES 24 BROWNIES

These seriously are the world's best brownies according to my son, and kids don't joke around when it comes to sweet matters. They are lighter than your average brownie, which I find can be a bit dense on occasion... I prefer mine fudgier and a bit lighter, more creamy, without feeling like you have eaten a brick. You can also make this recipe in a 8-inch round cake pan to create a brownie cake, which serves up as the most elegant and sophisticated soft centered chocolate cake for a grown-up dinner party. Just be sure to serve it with plenty of crème fraîche or sour cream, lightened with a bit of lemon and orange juice. I love to dust it with a little extra raw cacao powder if I am serving it as a dessert; a few fresh raspberries strewn over the top wouldn't go amiss either (just don't forget the crème fraîche!).

Scant 1¾ sticks unsalted butter (or ghee or coconut oil for a lactose-free version)

7 ounces best-quality dark chocolate

3 extra-large eggs

5½ tablespoons light honey

¾ cup coconut sugar

1 teaspoon vanilla extract

1 cup buckwheat flour

2 tablespoons arrowroot powder

½ teaspoon salt

Preheat the oven to 350°F. Line an 8-inch square baking pan with parchment paper.

Melt the butter and dark chocolate in a heavy-bottomed saucepan over medium–low heat.

Put the eggs in a bowl, and beat with the honey, coconut sugar, and vanilla.

Sift the flour and arrowroot into a separate bowl, and add the salt.

When the chocolate mixture has melted, take it off the heat and let it cool a little before beating in the egg mixture, and finally the flour mix.

Pour into the prepared baking pan, transfer to the middle rack of the oven, and bake for 18 minutes. You want the top to be cooked and hard, but when pushed very gently you should feel the soft and squidgy interior. They will cook a little more as they cool.

VARIATIONS

Salted honey caramel brownies.

1 quantity of honey salted caramel sauce taken to 271°F (see Variation on page 214) then cooled. Swirl half the mixture over the top of the brownies, and sprinkle with a little extra flaky salt. Bake for 20 minutes.

Nutty brownies.

"Activate" 1½ cups walnut halves by soaking in water for several hours or overnight (this reduces the phytates in the skin), then slowly drying until crispy again either in a dehydrator, or a slow oven. Stir the activated walnuts into the brownie mix, then bake for 20 minutes.

Raspberry brownies.

Stir through 5 ounces of fresh raspberries into the mixture, then bake for 20 minutes.

Rose and hazelnut brownies.

Add 2 teaspoons of rose water to the mixture, and sprinkle ⅜ cup toasted and roughly chopped hazelnuts over the top of the mix, then bake for 20 minutes.

Serve with crème fraîche, sweet kefir cream, or cashew mango cream (see pages 174 and 175).

The world's best
buckwheat brownies
(see page 207).

Honey salted
caramel sauce
(see page 214).

A simple meringue.

MAKES 1 LARGE PAVLOVA OR 6–10 NESTS

Meringues are an absolute delight, and no matter how many times I make them, they always feel like such an indulgent treat. Once you master the basic meringue, it's easy to adjust the toppings to create a seasonal masterpiece that will take center stage of any celebration, no matter the time of year. I have made meringues for dinner parties, birthday cakes, wedding cakes, bonfire parties, and lunchtime celebrations, and they always impress.

---

2 teaspoons apple cider vinegar

2 teaspoons cornstarch

6 egg whites

Pinch of salt

1 heaping cup organic golden superfine sugar

2 tablespoons maple syrup

1 teaspoon vanilla extract

Preheat the oven to 400°F.

Mix the vinegar and cornstarch in a small bowl, and stir until combined and lump-free.

Whisk the egg whites and salt in a large bowl until medium peaks form.

Using a free-standing cake mixer or hand-held electric whisk, very slowly add the sugar, 1 tablespoon at a time, alternating with a teaspoon of the vinegar mixture, whisking continuously until both are fully incorporated. This process should take about 10–12 minutes, by which time the meringue mix should be smooth, thick ,and glossy. Fold in the maple syrup and vanilla extract.

Line a baking tray with baking sheet, and stick the edges down by placing a blob of meringue under each corner.

For one large pavlova, draw a 10-inch circle on the baking parchment, spoon all the meringue into the circle, and neatly spread it with the back of a spoon or a palette knife into a large nest shape. If making smaller nests, place big dollops of meringue onto the sheet—you should get six to ten, depending on how large or small you want them.

Place the sheet in the oven and immediately turn the temperature down to 225°F.

Bake for about 2 hours for the smaller ones and 2½ hours for the larger size. You can turn the oven off and leave the meringue(s) in the oven overnight. If you are making them the same day you intend to eat them, just allow them to thoroughly cool before decorating.

To decorate, you will need 1 quantity of Chantilly cream (see page 173)—more if you like lots of cream—and then you can choose from one of the seasonal variations from the Perfect Sponge Cake recipe toppings on page 206, or whatever else you fancy. The meringues shown on the right have been decorated with roasted plums, finely chopped pistachios, and dried rose petals.

SWEET PANTRY   Sweet Butters and Creams   Nut Milks and Custard   Jams and Curds   Chocolate

Sweet spice mixes.

These delightful little sugar and spice mixes are perfect sprinkled over fruits before roasting, added to cream before whipping, or stirred into yogurt, and topped with your morning granola and fresh fruit. Add them to custard for a little twist, to fruit before you make a crumble topping, or to the topping itself if you like. They will perk up any baked goods if you add them before baking to crêpes, sponges, meringues, puddings, and tart crusts. Go wild.

Rose, cardamom, and coconut sugar spice mix.

MAKES 1 SMALL JAR

This is my favorite sweet spice mix, floral, but also earthy and deliciously fragrant. You either love cardamom or you hate it—I am definitely one of the former—and I also love the romantic scent and taste of rose, as long as it's not too overpowering.

This heavenly little mix would work very well for roasting plums, peaches, pears, blackberries, and also slow-baked rice puddings, custard tarts, baked custard, or even sprinkled over meringue nests filled with cream and fresh berries—heaven!

10 cardamom pods
2 tablespoons dried
  Damascan rose petals
½ cup coconut
  sugar

Dry-toast the cardamom pods in a skillet over medium–high heat until they are fragrant, and turning a very light brown color. Remove from the heat, and allow to cool for 5 minutes.

Place the pods, dried rose petals, and the sugar into a coffee or spice grinder, or use a mortar and pestle and grind until you have quite a fine powder.

Transfer to a glass jar with a tight-fitting lid, and keep in the cupboard until ready to use. This mix will last for a couple of months, but will diminish in flavor and fragrance as time goes by.

Sprinkle lightly over your favorite sweet things.

Vanilla, star anise, nutmeg, and cinnamon spice mix.

MAKES 1 SMALL JAR

This wonderfully heady and earthy-sweet spice mix is delicious paired with late summer fruits such as plums and hearty autumn and winter fruits, such as pears and apples.

1 star anise
½ cinnamon stick or
  1 tablespoon ground
  cinnamon
½ cup coconut sugar
4 teaspoons vanilla extract
½ nutmeg, finely grated

Place the star anise and cinnamon stick into a coffee or spice grinder. Grind until you have a fine powder, add the coconut sugar and grind again.

Mix the ground spices with the vanilla extract and the nutmeg. Mix, and then transfer to a glass jar with a tight-fitting lid, and keep in the cupboard until ready to use.

Vanilla and coconut sugar spice mix.

MAKES 1 SMALL JAR

4 teaspoons vanilla extract
6 tablespoons coconut sugar

Mix the ingredients in a small bowl, then transfer to a glass jar with a tight-fitting lid and keep in the cupboard until ready to use.

Honey salted caramel sauce.

MAKES ABOUT 1¼ CUPS

It doesn't get much better than honey salted caramel, it's the stuff of sweet dreams. Serve over ice cream, yogurt, crêpes, roasted pears, apples, bananas, custards or puddings, cakes and tarts, or drizzled over my favorite buckwheat brownies from page 207.

1¼ cups light honey, such as acacia or blossom honey
Generous ½ cup heavy cream
1 tablespoon unsalted butter
1 teaspoon vanilla extract or seeds of ½ vanilla bean

Generous 1–2 pinches of pink Himalayan salt, more if you would like the sauce quite salty

EQUIPMENT
Cooking thermometer

Pour the honey and cream into a medium saucepan, place it over medium–high heat, and stir until it reaches 262°F. Next stir in the butter, vanilla, and salt, whisking until the mixture becomes glossy and fully emulsified. Remove from the heat, and allow to cool a little. It will thicken as it cools. Use warm, drizzled over whatever you fancy; ice cream, or hot puddings, etc.

If you don't use it all immediately, keep in the fridge, and warm a little before serving to loosen.

Variation.
If you boil it down further, to roughly 271°F, it gets thicker and thicker on cooling, which would make it great for using in a caramel cookie bar... think layers of soft coconut, raw chocolate, and honey salted caramel... You could also add a little to smoothies to make raw cacao and honey salted caramel smoothies, with some frozen banana and raw whole milk or nutritious dairy-free raw homemade hazelnut milk from page 178, blitz it all in a high-powered blender with ice and voilà, honey salted caramel raw Ferrero Rocher smoothie—what could possibly be better?

Hot fudge sauce.

SERVES 4–6

This warm sauce is great drizzled over ice cream, puddings, roast fruit, crêpes... pretty much anything. Caramelized bananas would be incredible topped with this sauce and whipped cream to create a kind of grown-up banana split, sprinkled with a few toasted almond flakes for that necessary crunch.

Scant ¾ cup heavy cream (or coconut cream for a dairy-free option)
⅓ cup light honey
⅓ cup coconut sugar
3 tablespoons raw cacao powder
¼ teaspoon sea salt

6 ounces dark chocolate, roughly chopped, divided into 2 equal portions
2 tablespoons unsalted butter (or coconut butter for a dairy-free option)
1 teaspoon vanilla extract or seeds from 1 vanilla bean

Put the cream, honey, sugar, cacao powder, salt, and half the chocolate into a medium saucepan and heat over medium heat until it comes to a gentle boil. Immediately reduce the heat to a bare simmer, and cook for an additional 5–6 minutes, stirring occasionally with a wooden spoon.

Remove from the heat, and whisk in the remaining chocolate, the butter, and vanilla, stirring until velvety-smooth, glossy, and irresistible.

Set aside and allow it to cool and thicken a little before using. This takes about 20–30 minutes.

Store in a jar or glass bottle in the fridge for up to two weeks.

Warm gently in a pan before using to create a lovely smooth, warm sauce.

Blueberry and maple sauce.

MAKES 1–2 PINT JARS

This simple and wonderfully tasty little sauce is great on top of ice cream, crêpes, warm sponge cakes, granola and yogurt, and plenty besides. Blueberries are a fantastic gut-healing food, packed full of antioxidants, and they are juicy and delicious.

---

10 ounces blueberries, fresh or frozen, washed, and drained	⅞ cup maple syrup Juice of 1 lemon ¼ teaspoon vanilla extract

Put three-quarters of the blueberries in a medium saucepan with the maple syrup, half the lemon juice, and the vanilla. Bring to a boil, then turn down the heat and simmer for 10 minutes before adding the remaining blueberries, and lemon juice to taste. Simmer for an additional 2 minutes, or until thickened. Serve hot or cold. This delicious purple sauce will keep for a few days in the fridge.

Berry coulis.

SERVES 8

A berry coulis is great for drizzling over tarts, ice cream, sponges, crêpes, puddings, and other sweet delights. You could also drizzle it through homemade ice cream before freezing, to create a lovely swirl of color and extra flavor. It would also be wonderful used to make popsicles.

1½ pounds berries, such as raspberries or strawberries, or a mix Freshly squeezed juice of 1 lemon or lime	2½ tablespoons maple syrup or 3 tablespoons raw honey

Tip the fruit into a saucepan, mash lightly with a fork to release a few juices, and heat very gently to prevent scorching; you may need to add 1–2 teaspoons of water. Pop the lid on the pan just to encourage the fruit to start releasing its own juices. Simmer for 5–6 minutes, or until the fruit has lost its shape.

Blitz with a stick blender or in a food processor, then strain through a strainer to remove any tiny seeds and bits. Add the lemon or lime juice, also through a strainer, to taste. Add the maple syrup, and adjust sweetness or sourness to taste. Stir well, and transfer to the fridge to cool.

The coulis will keep in the fridge for up to one week.

VARIATIONS
Raspberry and rose coulis.
Use 1½ pounds of fresh or frozen raspberries, 1 teaspoon of rose water and the juice of 1 lemon. Follow the method above.

Strawberry and lime coulis.
Use 1½ pounds fresh or frozen strawberries, and use the juice of 1 or 2 limes, then follow the method above.

Syrups.

Making your own syrups is super-easy and well worth the effort, especially when you have a glut of fruit or the farmers' market or supermarket is overflowing with cheap berries. Berry syrups in particular are not only delicious, but packed full of vitamins, especially vitamin C, as is the hibiscus syrup, which makes them ideal for those cooler autumn months when an extra boost is just what we need to stave off those nasty seasonal bugs.

Hibiscus and raspberry syrup.

MAKES ABOUT 3⅓ CUPS

⅔ cup raw honey or brown
    rice syrup
Handful of dried hibiscus
    flowers

10 ounces raspberries, fresh
    or frozen

Put all the ingredients into a saucepan along with 3¼ cups water, and simmer very gently for about 20 minutes. Allow to cool a little, taste, and add more sweetener if necessary. Strain the mixture through a strainer, being careful not to let any of the bits get through. You can press the berries a bit to get as much liquid out of them as you can, but you don't want the pulp.

Pour the syrup into a glass bottle with a swing top. Store in the fridge. This syrup should last for a good week or so. Serve over ice and topped up with sparkling water.

As a refreshing non-alcoholic sparkling drink.

SERVES 1
2 handfuls crushed ice
⅓ glass of hibiscus and
    raspberry syrup

⅔ glass of sparkling water,
    plain kombucha, or water
    kefir
A few bruised mint or lemon
    verbena leaves

Half-fill a tall glass with crushed ice, pour over some syrup, about a third of the glass, then top up with sparkling water. Add a few bruised mint or lemon verbena leaves. Serve.

Hibiscus and crushed raspberry vodka cocktail.

SERVES 4–6
Crushed ice, enough to fill a
    1-quart jar half- to three-
    quarters full
7 ounces fresh raspberries,
    lightly crushed

⅓ jar of hibiscus and
    raspberry syrup (recipe
    above)
8 shots of good-quality vodka
About 3 cups soda water or
    plain kombucha

Fill the jar about three-quarters full with crushed ice, add the lightly crushed raspberries, and stir with a fork to mix into the ice. Pour in enough syrup to fill about one-third of the jar, add the vodka, and top up with soda water or kombucha. Top up with more ice if you need to.

Rhubarb, rose, and lime syrup.

MAKES ABOUT 3 1/3 CUPS

⅔ cup raw honey

5 forced pink rhubarb stalks,
   cut into small pieces

Juice of 3 limes

1 tablespoon rose water

Put 3¼ cups water in a small saucepan with the honey. Bring to a boil, and stir until the honey is completely dissolved. Remove from the heat, and pour into a glass pitcher and reserve.

Next put the rhubarb, lime juice, and rose water into the saucepan, and pour over just enough of the honey syrup to cover the rhubarb. Simmer very gently with a lid on, until the rhubarb is tender, but not totally disintegrated; this takes about 15–20 minutes. Allow to cool, then put the rhubarb mix through a strainer, with a bowl underneath to catch the liquid.

Mix the rhubarb syrup with the reserved honey syrup, stir, then transfer the entire batch of syrup into a clean glass bottle with a swing top.

Serve over ice, topped up with sparkling water.

As a refreshing non-alcoholic sparkling drink.

SERVES 1

Handful of crushed ice

⅓ glass chilled rhubarb, rose, and lime syrup

⅔ glass of sparkling water, plain kombucha or plain water kefir

A few dried rose petals, or fresh smaller-sized ones (optional)

1 forced rhubarb stalk, cut into lengths just a bit taller than the glass and then sliced into thin slices to create wide, flat slices

Half-fill a tall glass with crushed ice, pour over some syrup, about a third of the glass, then top up with sparkling water. Sprinkle over a few dried rose petals. Serve with a few of the thin strips of rhubarb in the drink for a beautiful effect, and extra zing.

Rhubarb, rose, and lime Prosecco cocktail.

SERVES 1

3 tablespoons chilled rhubarb, rose, and lime syrup

1 shot of good-quality chilled vodka (preferably straight from the freezer)

¾ glass Prosecco (or, for a less alcoholic version, plain kombucha)

1 fresh pink rose petal

Take a tall champagne flute, add the syrup and vodka, stir lightly together, and top up with prosecco. Garnish with a fresh rose petal and serve.

Blueberry and blackberry syrup.

MAKES ABOUT 3⅓ CUPS

1¼ cups raw honey

6 ounces blackberries

6 ounces blueberries

Juice of ½ lemon

Handful of elderberries
(optional, if in season)

Put 3¼ cups water in a small saucepan with the honey. Bring to a boil, and stir until the honey is completely dissolved. Remove from the heat, and pour into a glass pitcher and reserve.

Next, place the berries and lemon juice into the saucepan, and pour over just enough of the syrup to cover the berries. Cover the pan with a lid, and simmer very gently until the berries are tender, but not totally disintegrated; this takes about 15 minutes. Allow to cool, then put the berries through a strainer, with a bowl underneath to catch the liquid. Discard the pulp, or keep it to add to yogurt.

Mix the berry syrup with the reserved honey syrup, stir, then transfer the batch of syrup into a clean glass bottle with a swing top.

As a refreshing non-alcoholic sparkling drink.

SERVES 1

2 handfuls crushed ice

⅓ glass blueberry and
blackberry syrup

⅔ glass sparkling water, plain
kombucha, or water kefir

A few bruised mint or lemon
verbena leaves

A squeeze of lime juice

Half-fill a tall glass with crushed ice, pour over some syrup, about one-third of the glass, then top up with sparkling water. Add a few bruised mint or lemon verbena leaves. Serve.

Blueberry and blackberry vodka cocktail.

SERVES 1

2 handfuls of crushed ice

¼ glass of blueberry and
blackberry syrup

1 or 2 shots of good-quality
vodka

¾ glass of soda water or plain
kombucha

1 wedge of lime

A few borage flowers or
a purple viola flower
(optional)

Half-fill a tall glass with crushed ice, pour over the syrup, add the vodka, stir, then top up with soda water. Take the wedge of lime, squeeze over the drink, then add the wedge to the glass. Top with borage flowers or a purple viola, if any are available.

Index.

Index.

Index.

Acknowledgements.

Firstly I would would like to thank Kyle, my wonderful publisher, for her amazing support. She has been with me all the way with her wonderful encouragement and patience. She has always believed in me, and has given me the push when I needed it. So thank you Kyle for your amazing help and support along the way. I would also like to thank Tara at Kyle Books, my editor, for her wonderful support and hard work to get this book finished. It's been a cross-continental marathon and it's only ever been a joy to work with her. She has helped me to achieve the vision that I had for this book, which has been a wonderful experience. Thank you for all your hard work and talent at keeping the bigger vision on track.

Nassima Rothacker, my amazing and talented photographer, has gone so far above and beyond the call of duty I honestly don't know where I would have been without her. Nassima has given her time and talent and eye for beauty all the way through, so thank you from the bottom of my heart for all your amazing help Nassima. You are quite simply a legend, and a talented, gorgeous one at that!!

Thanks also to Jacqui Porter for your wonderful design and hard work. It's been a lovely process working with you and seeing the book come to life.

Thank you to my wonderful agent, Amanda Preston, you have helped to keep me on the straight and narrow, and bouncing ideas off you has been a pleasure. Your guidance has been invaluable.

I also want to thank Carly at Establishment Studios. She was so helpful and working and shooting in those heavenly rooms was a dream. Also, thanks Carly for all the early morning car rides through beautiful sunny Melbourne.

Thanks to Kirsty Bryson for her stunning props, and local knowledge of food markets and tips on where to find rare and beautiful things. The book wouldn't have looked the same without all your treasures. Thank you to Lynda Gardener, working with you and shooting in your amazing house, The Estate Trentham, was quite simply a dream come true. Your amazing style made the book what it is. I don't think a more stunning location exists, I only wish I had more time to luxuriate in those heavenly linen sheets looking out onto the garden on the misty Trentham mornings.

Thanks also to Aleta and Isabella at Vitamix Australia/New Zealand for lending me one of your superb machines. My silky-smooth nut butters and creamy, dreamy nut milks would not have been the same without the amazing Vitamix that you sent.

A special thanks to the amazing people at Lavandula, a stunning lavender farm just outside Melbourne. Thanks for letting us sneak in at daybreak and shoot our sunrise shots in the lavender fields.

Thanks also to Tom and Michael, my food styling assistant and my photographer's assistant, who gave both Nassima and I many laughs, and an endless stream of delicious iced Melbourne coffees on those hot summer days when the pace was fast and a little extra boost was needed. You supported us with humor and hard work, thank you both so much!!

I would also like to thank my gorgeous friends Emma Bishop and Cass, and their gorgeous and funny twins Sadie and Scout, for putting up with me blocking your entire hallway with bags of shopping as far as the eye could see—and for leaving out delicious meals for me when I was working late into the night, and didn't have the energy to walk another step, let alone feed myself. I miss you so much, and it was amazing to spend that time with you.

Thanks to Kerry Wilson and Richard Lewer for lending me your house; it was my cool, calm little oasis in a very hot Melbourne city, hanging with your cats in the garden, and hosing myself down under the garden hose while picking arugula from your garden was pure heaven. Thanks also to Kerry for helping me to achieve some backstreet Kefir deals, an experience I shall never forget.

Thank you to Christine Newman for being the perfect aunty, driving me all around Melbourne and helping to load about a thousand bags of shopping into your car, fridge, house, back to the car, and all around town. Couldn't have pulled it off without you. You are a legend!

Thank you to my darling delicious friends, India Waters, Beshlie McKelvie, and Natalie Ferstendik. I miss you all, and thank you from the bottom of my heart for your endless creative inspiration that you all give in every way, as beautiful mothers, artists, creators, and lovers of life. I love you all.

Thank you to Oma, Grattan, Ed, Ben, Annabel, and Nicola Guinness for all your patience and support in helping me to get this book over the line. Your love of food, and pure enjoyment in eating has always been a huge inspiration to me.

Thank you to Lucinda, Orson, and Evie, I love you all, and can't wait for more adventures. Thanks for always being amazing and wonderful.

Lastly I would like to thank my wonderful family. Mum, Bob, Aunty Rach, Aunty Viv, Aunty Marion, my wonderful Brother Taiamai and Franzi and my family who live in Oz, Aaron, Kylie, and Rana and all their beautiful children. I wouldn't be who I am today without the adventures we shared, and the support that I have received over the years. Thanks To Maida for creating us all, I hope your 90th will be the best year yet!

A special thanks to my darling son Oli. Everything I do is for you; the early mornings, the late nights, the hard graft and the digging deep. I hope that I can inspire you in your life to follow your dreams as my mother inspired me to follow mine. I love you more than the moon and the stars.

Published in 2017 by Kyle Books
www.kylebooks.com

Distributed by National Book Network
4501 Forbes Blvd, Suite 200,
Lanham, MD 20706
Phone: (800) 462-6420
Fax: (800) 338-4550
customercare@nbnbooks.com

First published in Great Britain in 2016
by Kyle Books, an imprint of Kyle Cathie Ltd

10 9 8 7 6 5 4 3 2 1

ISBN 978 1 909487 65 9

Project Editor: Tara O'Sullivan
Editorial Assistant: Amberley Lowis
Copy Editor: Stephanie Evans
Editorial Adaptation: Lee Faber
Designer: Jacqui Porter, Northwood Green
Photographer: Nassima Rothacker
Food and Props Stylist: Amber Rose
Production: Nic Jones and Gemma John

Library of Congress Control Number: 2017941791

Color reproduction by ALTA London
Printed and bound in China by 1010 International Printing Ltd.